So, You to be an International Baccalaureate School, Eh?

SE Publications:
Great Falls, Montana
USA

Edward L. Varner, M.Ed.

SE Publications

A Subdivision of Spaghetti Eddie Productions
PO BOX 1628
Great Falls, Montana 59403-1628
Telephone 1-406-788-2743

Acknowledgements

To my family: Wife and partner, Christiana; daughters, Megan and Taylor; and son, Sean-Edward. Thank you for your support, for loving me, and for putting up with so much dabbling in various projects.

I'd like to acknowledge and thank the mentorship and guidance of Dr. Dan Brown from the University of British Columbia and Ron Brown from the North Vancouver school District for helping to facilitate this project.

Thank you to my research colleagues Suzette Buchanan, Leanne Douglas, Karim Hachlaf, and Peter Williams of the University of British Columbia Educational Leadership and Administration cohort and all the participants who generously donated time to this project.

Gratitude and appreciation beyond words to Christiana Rennie-Varner, MA for her editing and sensible approach to the required paradigm shift that education needs and for guiding me out of the box.

Contents

Chapter 1

So, you want to be an International Baccalaureate School, eh?

So, you think you want an International Baccalaureate Programme at your school? You are not alone. Many school districts around the world are considering the adoption of K-12 International Baccalaureate Programmes. Clearly, when looking at changes of this magnitude, it is useful to evaluate other schools and school districts that have implemented similar programs. What exactly are the strengths and weaknesses of a K-12 International Baccalaureate Programme? As an educator and parent, I wanted to know how IB could affect schools. So I undertook a study to determine the academic, economic, political, cultural, and physical impact an International Baccalaureate programme has on a school. In general, I liked what I found.

In January of 2005 I began an investigation into the world of the International Baccalaureate. My research adventure started with a review of current research literature related to the International Baccalaureate Programme. From this search I found that the enterprise of the International Baccalaureate Programmes grew out of the practical and educational concerns of international schools as they endeavored to meet the needs of university bound students. Originally, international school authorities recognized a dilemma faced by their university bound students as they prepared for regional exams and requirements while also preparing for entrance exams from the world's leading universities. Mobile international students were often at a disadvantage due to inconsistencies and discrepancies in the diverse programmes offered by various international schools. The International

Baccalaureate Organization (IBO) was founded in an attempt to address these and other needs related to a mobile, international community of students. The process has been referred to as "an interesting experiment in international education" that has grown to an established and widely recognized university entrance qualification (Bagnal, 1997, pg. 18).

It quickly became quite evident that the International Baccalaureate Programme opens new academic avenues for students and is a programme of considerable interest to many public schools. Do International Baccalaureate Programs meet the academic needs of students and are they really as good as we think they are? Are International Baccalaureate Programmes worth the inevitable student, teacher, and budgetary stress that accompany a programme of this magnitude? In an effort to shed some light on these questions, I and a team of researchers from the University of British Columbia examined the International Baccalaureate Programmes at Britannia Secondary Community School and Sir Winston Churchill Secondary School in Vancouver, British Columbia. We interviewed and surveyed the administrators, teachers, and parents involved in the IB programme and we observed a significant amount of enthusiasm for the IB program at these schools. The findings of our research study demonstrated that International Baccalaureate Programs do, in fact, meets the needs of those exceptional students who require a more challenging curriculum and are self-motivated to succeed. The programme definitely meets the academic needs of students. It meets and or exceeds local requirements for promotion and provides a more than adequate preparation for entrance into leading universities. The programme offers equal opportunity to all self-motivated and academically capable students. In fact, one hundred percent of the teachers surveyed agreed that the programme

meets the local requirements for promotion and provides solid preparation for university entrance.

Despite the emerging evidence that the International Baccalaureate Programme is a positive element for a host school, my research team found a significant lack of understanding about the impact, potential benefits, and potential pitfalls of the programme among key stakeholders. Many respondents to our study were unclear of the academic requirements for International Baccalaureate students. There was considerable discrepancy between answers to similar questions regarding the needs and requirements of IB schools and students. Participants were uncertain if the programme better met the needs of students than other programs such as Advanced Placement (AP). While all participants were very positive and confident that the programme was a good one, they often had a difficult time articulating why.

The impact of the International Baccalaureate programme on the students, staff, and school was multifaceted. The findings of our project indicated that there is evidence of strong leadership, motivation, competitiveness, and cliques among students in the International Baccalaureate Programme. It also showed that students who are currently involved in the programme express evidence of a vested, strong interest in it. Similarly, the findings showed that there is strong interest from other students in the school about the International Baccalaureate Programme. Currently at the study schools (Britannia Secondary Community School and Sir Winston Churchill Secondary School), pre-IB programmes are offered for grade 10 students with an interest in the programme. This practice appears to attract interested students to the school. The findings clearly indicated that the atmosphere in schools with International Baccalaureate Programmes is positive and learning based; that teachers teaching in the International Baccalaureate Programme are enthusiastic about the courses and the International Baccalaureate Programme in general and have a strong belief that the programme addresses the needs of students who desire an academic challenge. Teachers felt that the programme is of benefit to the general population of the school as well, in setting high expectations and standards, and instilling an academic based focus in the school. Overall, I reached the following conclusions about the International Baccalaureate Programme.

International Baccalaureate Programmes meet local aims of education.

The British Columbia Ministry of Education states that the purpose of the British Columbia school system is to enable learners to develop their individual potential and to acquire the knowledge, skills and attitudes needed to contribute to a healthy society and a prosperous and sustainable economy (www.bced.gov.bc.ca/mission.htm, April 28, 2005). The International Baccalaureate Programme fits within this provincial goal. It is a complete and rigorous curriculum designed to prepare students for entrance into the world's leading universities. International Baccalaureate students are being accepted into post-secondary institutions at a much higher rate than non-IB students. The principal purpose of the programme is to provide students with a balanced, integrated curriculum that focuses on all academic areas (IBO and the College Board, 2002). The results showed that parents (97%) and teachers (100%) agree that the programme provides a challenging curriculum.

Parents (75%) and teachers (67%) also agree that courses in the programme require university level work that meets and surpasses the requirements of their local school boards of education and the Provincial Curriculum. In order to receive an International Baccalaureate Diploma, students must take and pass world standard exams in six subject areas, fulfill a community service requirement, submit an extended essay, and follow an interdisciplinary course in Theory of Knowledge.

The Primary Years Program and the Middle Years Programme are early in their development and, as a result, have few definitive studies of evaluation to support them. The limited literature suggests that both programmes adequately meet the academic needs of students (Singh, 2002, p.1).

International Baccalaureate programs meet the academic needs of students.

My research study agrees with current literature and suggests that International Baccalaureate Programmes at the high school level do indeed meet the academic requirements of students (Bagnal, 1997, Pajak 2000, and Osborn, 1999). Parents responded with 80% agreement and teachers responded overwhelmingly with 99% that the International Baccalaureate Programme meets the academic needs of students

The International Baccalaureate Programme offers a credible and strong alternative for students.

My results revealed a consensus among the teacher participants on the ability of the International Baccalaureate to offer challenging coursework, specialized courses, a focus on skill development, and an opportunity for university credit. All of these areas can be characterized as good educational practice (Pajak, 2000). Furthermore, my interview respondents from both Britannia Secondary and Churchill Secondary favorably described the International Baccalaureate programme. The programme offers an additional choice for students looking to pursue a more rigorous academic curriculum that would better prepare them for post secondary education.

There are many levels of accountability in an International Baccalaureate.

The primary objective of the International Baccalaureate Programme is to provide students with a balanced, integrated curriculum in all academic areas. Students who excel in the International Baccalaureate Programme demonstrate a strong commitment to learning and develop the discipline necessary to succeed later in life. Students in the International Baccalaureate Programme are responsible for making a commitment to the programme, developing international understanding and demonstrating responsible citizenship. Students in the programme are personally accountable for their studies and success in the programme.

Teachers working in the International Baccalaureate Programme are accountable on two different levels. First, they are responsible for taking additional courses, workshops and professional development provided by the International Baccalaureate Organization. This training allows the teachers to become knowledgeable about the expectations, curriculum, and methodology prescribed by the International Baccalaureate Organization. Second, teachers are accountable for teaching the curriculum laid out by the IBO, and adequately preparing their students for the International Baccalaureate exams in each of the six subject areas.

At the school level, the IB team is accountable on many different levels. The team is accountable for student admissions, scheduling of courses, hiring staff, teacher training, and the daily running of the programme. In addition they are responsible for ensuring the internal assessment of student work, liaising with parent and community, and the proper preparation of students for exams.

International Baccalaureate Programmes worldwide are also accountable to the International Baccalaureate Organization (IBO). The IBO provides International Baccalaureate schools with detailed curriculum guidelines for each programme and subject area. They also provide teacher training workshops. In addition, the IBO completes external assessment of diploma students' work, and procedures for school-based (internal) assessment of student work. The IBO is also responsible for the administration and grading of IBO examinations. The grading system for the exams is criterion-referenced. This means that each student's performance is measured against well-defined levels of achievement. Top grades reflect knowledge and skills relative to set standards applied equally to all schools. Responsibility for all academic judgments about the quality of students' work rests with over 5,000 examiners worldwide, led by chief examiners with international authority in their fields. At another level the IBO works closely with schools throughout the initial authorization process by offering introductory workshops and supplying schools with application forms. During the process of implementing an International Baccalaureate Programme, which is required for authorization, the IBO advises schools on the materials that they will need and offer teacher training workshops and conferences (IBO, 2004).

IB Programmes can co-exist in a school with a provincial curriculum.

This research project confirmed that there is a definite impact upon the students and the school by the International Baccalaureate Programme. The host schools were affected with an increased overall academic achievement and increased resources.

When considering the effects of student segregation due to the International Baccalaureate, the findings of this study suggested 70% of teachers disagreed that this was the case while parents were undecided. There were numerous opportunities for International Baccalaureate students to participate in school wide leadership opportunities and to be involved with the daily activities of the general student population. The curriculum provides avenues for students to become involved and play major roles in areas like student council. Parents were undecided on this matter while the limited literature suggested that there was no policy that would actually create a segregated type of setting.

Recommendations for Research and Practice

My research questions were all answered with positive responses regarding the International Baccalaureate Programme. Based upon my analysis, I support the idea of implementing the International Baccalaureate programme. However, there are some important considerations to make before making a commitment to the implementation of the programme.

The majority of individuals involved in International Baccalaureate Programmes in the two schools studied are strong supporters of the programme. Clearly, the International Baccalaureate is a good option for the gifted population. It meets the academic needs of an underserved segment of the student population, but it is not a program for all students or teachers. Interested districts should conduct further research in the Primary and Middle Years Programmes, International Baccalaureate Programmes in other districts, and other academic programmes like Advanced Placement before making a final decision.

Districts considering an International Baccalaureate Programme should conduct an in depth study on the actual classroom needs of an International Baccalaureate Programme. It would be valuable to schools to have access to a specific list of teacher, student, and building requirements prior to beginning the process of becoming an International Baccalaureate school. Additionally, a comparison of an International Baccalaureate classroom and a provincially examinable classroom should be conducted. Through this comparison, schools could look at whether the teaching styles differ greatly from one classroom to the next. This examination would allow schools and districts to come to a conclusion about whether or not the training for International Baccalaureate teachers is helpful and a worthwhile expenditure.

Advanced Placement and International Baccalaureate Programmes ought to be compared. This additional study would determine if one program is better to local implementation and marketing than the other. A combined study of International Baccalaureate graduates and individuals who have dropped out or withdrawn from the programme ought to be performed. As a result, the effect of stress and burnout on International Baccalaureate participants could possibly be determined.

This and subsequent chapters of this text are based on Suzette Buchanan, Leanne Douglas, Karim Hachlaf, Peter Williams, and Edward Varner's (2005) *Evaluating the International Baccalaureate Programme: An IB Proposal for the Consideration of the North Vancouver School District.* Unpublished Graduating Paper, Educational Administration and Leadership Program, Department of Educational Studies, Faculty of Education, University of British Columbia, Vancouver, B.C. 136 pp.

Resources

Bangall, N. (1997) Un Mariage de convenance! The
       International Baccalaureate and the French
       Baccalaureat Professionel. What Chance of a
       Union. *International Education-e*. 3, 17-21.
       Retrieved November 4, 2004 from
       http://www.services.canberra.edu
International Baccalaureate Organization and the College
Board. (2002). *Informational Brochure on IB and AP*.
Retrieved October 31, 2004 from
       http://www.ibo.org/ibo/index.cfm?contentid=0000E
614-48A3-1DD5-
       8E1280C12645FD37&method=display&language=
EN

International Baccalaureate Organization (2004). *A basis
       for Practice: the Primary Years Programme*.
       Retrieved October 31, 2004 from
       http://www.ibo.org/ibo/index.cfm?contentid=7EB3
       9840-C56F-98A0-
       67A9C7127EAD217D&method=display&language
       =EN
Pajak, E. (2000). *Approaches to clinical supervision:
       alternatives for improving instruction*. Norwood,
       MA: Christopher-Gordon Publishers, Inc.
Singh, N. (2002). Becoming International. *Educational
       Leadership*, 60, 5p. Retrieved September 21, 2004,
       from EBSCO Research Database
       http://web14.epnet.com/citation.asp

Chapter 2
Welcome to the World of IB: An Introduction to the International Baccalaureate

The enterprise of the International Baccalaureate Programmes appears to have grown out of the practical and educational concerns of international schools as they endeavored to meet the needs of university bound students. Originally, international school authorities recognized a dilemma faced by their university bound students as they prepared for regional exams and requirements while also preparing for entrance exams from the worlds leading universities. Mobile international students were often at a disadvantage due to inconsistencies and discrepancies in the diverse programmes offered by various international schools. The International Baccalaureate Organization (IBO) was founded in an attempt to address these and other needs related to a mobile, international community of students. The process has been referred to as "an interesting experiment in international education" that has grown to an established and widely recognized university entrance qualification (Bagnal, 1997, pg. 18).

History and Description of the International Baccalaureate Programmes

The International Baccalaureate Organization was founded in Geneva, Switzerland in 1969 as a non-profit educational organization. The initial purpose of the International Baccalaureate Organization was to facilitate the educational needs of internationally mobile students by preparing a curriculum and diploma programme that would be recognized by universities around the world. Since its origin, the International Baccalaureate Organization has expanded offerings to include the original International

Baccalaureate Diploma Programme (IBDP) for students ages 16 to 19 (grades 11 and 12), the Middle Years Programme (MYP) for ages 11 to 16, and the Primary Years Programme (PYP) for students ages 3 to 12. The International Baccalaureate Organization presents the complete programme as a sequential curriculum that promotes the education of the "whole person, emphasizing intellectual, personal, and social growth, through all domains of knowledge, involving the major traditions of learning in languages, humanities, sciences, mathematics, and the arts" (www.ibo.org).

The newest addition to the International Baccalaureate Organization's programme offerings is the Primary Years Programme (PYP). The Primary Years Programme was introduced in September of 1997 and completes the philosophical concept of "an educational continuum... of a consistent, broad-based international curriculum" (www.ibo.org). The programme attempts to produce students who represent the attributes of an ideal international person. In this regard, defining the attributes of an international person creates a significant amount of difficulty.

The Primary Years Programme suggests that by creating a profile of the 10 most important attributes of an international person, teachers and schools can respond better to the question, "What do we want students to learn" (Singh, 2002, p.1)? In addition to the curricular definition provided by the International Baccalaureate Organization, Singh suggests that international students should "learn how to be inquirers, thinkers, communicators, risk takers, knowledgeable, principled, caring, open-minded, and reflective" (Singh, 2002, p.1). The Primary Years Programme then focuses each part of the curriculum on moving students toward becoming young people who are representative of these characteristics. The specifics of how the International Baccalaureate curriculum achieves this goal are clouded by the licensing and training requirements of the International Baccalaureate Organization, but its essence can be gleaned by Singh's description in the text *Becoming International*:

> The Primary Years Programme defines six themes that transcend the traditional disciplines and represent broad ideas that are relevant to, and meaningful for, all human beings: who we are, where we are in place and time, how we express ourselves, how the world works, how we organize ourselves, and sharing the planet. Each year of elementary school, about half of class time is spent exploring these six themes, with 4-6 weeks spent on each unit. Much of the content that teachers have always taught- that they are in many cases required to teach- works naturally into the units, although the instructional approach changes quite dramatically. After all, students around the world learn about igloos, tepees, mud huts, and homes on stilts for a reason. The Primary Years Programme simply encourages teachers to emphasize, for example, the core concept that human beings need shelter. Examining different kinds of homes then become a means to an end rather than the end of the lesson (Singh, 2002, p.2).

Essentially, the Primary Years Programme is a structured guideline for elementary schools to use as a vehicle for learning. The Primary Years Programme uses trans-disciplinary themes to help teachers and students explore knowledge in broad terms amongst multiple disciplines. The programme utilizes a core set of concept based questions in order to help structure units of inquiry. Table 1.1 identifies the programme's trans-disciplinary themes and core set of concept questions. In addition to the trans-disciplinary themes and the core concepts, the development of language (both native language and an additional second language) and attitudes of socially responsible behavior are key elements of the programme.

Table 1.1
Trans-disciplinary themes and concepts

Trans-disciplinary themes	Core set of concepts
Who we are	Form: What is it like?
Where we are in place and time	Function: How does it work?
How we express ourselves	Causation: Why is it changing?
How the world works	Change: How is it changing?
How we organize ourselves	Connection: How is it connected to other things?
Sharing the planet	Perspective: What are the points of view?
	Responsibility: What is our responsibility?
	Reflection: How do we know?

Adapted from www.ibo.org

While the Primary Years Programme serves as an introduction to the Middle Years Programme (MYP), it is not a prerequisite. Similarly, the Middle Years Programme is not a requirement for the International Baccalaureate Diploma Programme. They do, however both spend a significant amount of effort identifying and defining the attributes of an international person. The goal of the programme is to develop students who are "inquirers, thinkers, communicators, risk takers, knowledgeable, principled, caring, and open minded" (Singh, 2002, p. 5).

The Middle Years Programme, introduced in 1994, provides a framework of academic study for students aged 11 – 16. The programme accents and advocates the interrelatedness of a thorough study of a wide variety of disciplines. By establishing assessment criteria for teachers, the International Baccalaureate Organization's 5 year programme encourages schools to exceed traditional school subjects and requirements as they prepare students for high school. This programme, like the Primary Years Programme, is new to the offerings of the International Baccalaureate Organization and as such, is largely unproven. The Primary Years Programme and the Middle Years Programme are presented by the International Baccalaureate Organization as solid structures for the foundations of education. They both encourage the development of language and internationalism with the International Baccalaureate Organization providing support material for a global curriculum.

The International Baccalaureate Organization's original programme, created in 1968, is a well documented and generally respected course of study that leads to university acceptable entrance examinations for students age 16-19. It is a two-year programme offered in English, French, and Spanish and is the most clearly defined of the three programmes offered by the International Baccalaureate Organization. The programme was established in an effort to create a common curriculum to meet the needs of internationally mobile secondary students that would emphasize critical thinking, intercultural understanding, and offer exposure to a variety of viewpoints while preparing students to attend world universities (Sigh, 2002; Paris, 2003; IBO website, 2004).

The International Baccalaureate Diploma Programme (IBDP) calls for students to successfully participate in the study of languages, sciences, mathematics, and humanities at the honours level during their final 2 years of secondary education. The intent of the programme is that students should learn how to learn, analyze, reach considered conclusions about people, languages and literature, society, and the scientific forces of the world environment. In order to receive an International baccalaureate Diploma, a student must successfully pass an exam from each of the 6 areas listed in table 1.2 (language A & B, individuals and society, science, mathematics, and the arts). The International Baccalaureate Diploma requires at least 3 but not more than 4 exams at the higher level. Courses ranked at the higher level (HL) require a minimum of 240 minutes of instructional time in class while courses ranked at the Standard level (SL), occasionally referred to as the subsidiary level, require a minimum of 150 minutes of instructional time.

Area 1	Language A: The primary language of the school including world literature	The IBO offers examinations for more than 80 languages. Students develop strong written and oral skills and a respect for the literary traditions of their primary language.
Area 2	Language B: Second language	The courses in this area focus on written and spoken communication in a second language. Latin and Greek are also available in group 2.
Area 3	Individuals and Society: History	Examples from this area include: business and management, economics, geography, history, information technology in a global society, philosophy, psychology, and social and cultural anthropology.
Area 4	Experimental Sciences	Examples from this area include: biology, chemistry, physics, environmental systems, and design technology.
Area 5	Mathematics and Computer Science	Courses in this area aim to deepen student understanding mathematics as a discipline and to promote confidence and facility in the use of mathematical language. Computer science is an elective subject in area 5.
Area 6	The Arts	This area includes visual arts, music and theatre arts, with emphasis placed on practical production and exploration.

Table 1.2 *The Six Content Areas of the International Baccalaureate Diploma Programme*
Adapted from www.ibo.org

The initial goals of the International Baccalaureate Diploma came from a need to assist international students attain equal footing into world universities and not to realize the educational needs of every student in every part of the world. This original intention and purpose of the programme is a concern when school districts are taking into consideration the adoption of an International Baccalaureate programme. Additionally, a review of pertinent literature identifies some concerns about the homogenization of ideas and values that could potentially lead to the loss of existing diverse local ideas and values. How does an International Baccalaureate Programme fit into the local aim or goal of education? Will it meet the needs of local students? These are questions that require measured exploration and consideration (Paris, 2003). They will be addressed in the literature review after a brief look at the target district from this study.

Snapshot of North Vancouver School District

North Vancouver is comprised of the Corporation of the City of North Vancouver (population 44,000) and the Corporation of the District of North Vancouver (population 83,000). The North Vancouver School District (NVSD) has 18,500 students enrolled in Kindergarten through Grade 12 throughout the City and District. There are twenty nine elementary schools, two alternate schools, and seven secondary schools which deliver a comprehensive K-12 education programme consisting of over 200 provincial and locally developed educational programmes and services. The programmes and services have been designed to provide all students with the courses necessary to enter university, college, or other post-secondary education. In North Vancouver schools are organized into "families of schools" with each of the seven secondary schools serving a geographical "catchment" area made up of a number of feeder elementary schools.

The North Vancouver School District currently offers many alternatives to students in the district. These alternatives include French Immersion, the Youth and Family Programme, the Youth Learning Centre, Eslah7an, Learning Together, Third Step, Windsor House, and the Keith Lynn Programme. Alternative programmes often offer smaller class settings and additional individual attention than those offered in traditional settings. These programmes offer settings which stress the individuality of the learner and focus on the strengths of the individual (North Vancouver School District, 2004).

The North Vancouver School District has projected an operating budget deficit of $7.5 million for the next three years (North Vancouver School District, 2004). Several ideas for overcoming this deficit were proposed at a community forum held in November 2003. The proposals included ideas for generating additional revenue via the creation of magnet schools offering programmes such as the International Baccalaureate (North Vancouver School District, 2003). The topic of the possible implementation of an International Baccalaureate Programme as a way to generate extra revenue was explored again at a community forum in October 2004. There appears to be an interest by parents, teachers, and community members for an International Baccalaureate Programme in North Vancouver.

Research Questions and Rationale for the study

This study examines the various International Baccalaureate Programmes in order to help North American schools, specifically the North Vancouver School District in British Columbia, Canada, make informed decisions when considering the adoption and implementation of International Baccalaureate

Programmes.   The research attempts to answer the question: Do International Baccalaureate Programmes meet the academic needs of North American students and schools?   The study ventures into some of the motivating factors surrounding the consideration of International Baccalaureate Programmes.   In considering motivating factors for International Baccalaureate implementation, the research attempts to answer the following questions:

> Do International Baccalaureate Programmes meet the academic needs of North American students and schools?
>
> How does the International Baccalaureate Programme fit into the local aim or goal of education?
>
> Is the notion of 'best practice' the driving philosophy behind the initiative?
>
> Is the driving force behind the implementation of an International Baccalaureate Programme solely that of attracting students (money) to the school district?
>
> What measures of accountability are enforced in an International Baccalaureate school?
>
> What are the affects of an International Baccalaureate Programme on student populations?

As educators consider various rallying points for change there becomes an evident need for unbiased, research-based information for the purposes of guiding and directing change.   It is here that this study hopes to add valuable information for those districts considering the implementation of an International Baccalaureate Programme for their students.   "Decisions are rational if there is a reasonable connection between the means and ends" and therefore "if decision makers choose wisely the appropriate means for advancing their goals" (Hoy and

Tarter, 2004, p. 3). For the purposes in this evaluation of an International Baccalaureate Programme, I ask the question: do the academic and economic gains of an International Baccalaureate Programme significantly justify and connect to the means necessary to implement the programme? I am hopeful that the information contained in this study will aid in this decision making process. The economic cost as related to academic gains will be addressed later in chapter three. At this point, however, it does seem appropriate to scrutinize various ways in which the International Baccalaureate Programme satisfies the various rallying points for change that public schools are experiencing. In the text *Approaches to Clinical Supervision: Alternatives for Improving Instruction,* Pajak suggests that the first call for change revolves around the challenges created by "a technologically sophisticated global economy..." and the notion that "each nation's economic competitiveness in today's knowledge based world depends primarily in its schools to prepare knowledgeable, self disciplined individuals who... possess strong analytical, interpersonal, and communication skills" (Pajak, p. 9). Is the International Baccalaureate Programme a programme that is beneficial for schools attempting to meet this challenge?

Chapter 3
What does the Literature say about the International Baccalaureate?

There has been little unbiased academic research into the merit and evaluation of the International Baccalaureate Program. In this chapter I attempt to outline some of the limited literature available as it relates to the questions that arise when evaluating and considering an educational program of this scope. The chapter begins with two subsections offering information on the academic elements of the program and how they support the aims of western education. The review will investigate the program from both qualitative and quantitative points of view in order to assess the thoroughness of International Baccalaureate Programmes and their ability to address the academic needs of students and society.

In addition to evaluating and comparing the International Baccalaureate and other advanced academic programs such as AP (Advanced Placement), I will focus on political and economic elements and ramifications associated with the programme. These subsequent sections of the chapter will examine the potential consequences and needs of an implemented International Baccalaureate Programme. Issues of choice, teacher unions, staffing dilemmas, and funding concerns will be attend to as they relate to the requirements of an International Baccalaureate Programme. The chapter will conclude with issues of school culture, the physical plant requirements, and culminating thoughts for consideration when considering the implementation of an International Baccalaureate Programme.

An Academic Perspective

Do International Baccalaureate Programmes meet the academic needs of North American students and schools? In order to address this question, I'll first examine the academic debate to determine what North America, specifically Canada and the United States, view as important in elementary-secondary education. I'll then compare these goals and objectives of public education in North America with the International model presented by the International Baccalaureate Organization and determine if the International Baccalaureate model meets and or exceeds the objectives sought by schools in North America. Or, does the International Baccalaureate model fall short?

A 1988 British Columbia Royal Commission on education addressed the four purposes for schooling: "the cultivation of the mind, preparation for vocational life, moral and civic development, and individual development" (Osborn, 1999, p. 24). In 1994 a Royal Commission on Learning in Ontario narrowed and defined the purpose of schooling to three primary objectives: to make certain all students achieve a high level of literacy (basic reading, writing, and problem solving across a variety of subject areas), the development in students of a desire to continue learning through out life, and the preparation of students for responsible citizenship. The focus on responsible citizenship included the development of the moral values of compassion, respect, anti-racism, peace, non-violence, honesty, and justice. Osborn suggests that the various points of the debate for most North Americans, regardless of political philosophies of education, boil down to the expectation that schools will convey knowledge, skills, and values to their students. Schools are also expected to impart the values of democracy to students in North American schools (Osborn, 1999).

"Preparing students to live in a technologically sophisticated, information based, global society..." (Pajak,

2000, p. 291) is a challenging task that enters the debate about how schools are to educate students. One of the many factors challenging education today is the fact that students are extremely diverse in their cultures, languages, and past experiences. Pajak argues that education is more than a system for transferring knowledge, skills, and culture from one generation to the next, but in fact it is more essentially a system for inventing and reinventing knowledge, skills, and culture. He suggests a liberal position that educators must commit to the democratic values of equality, participation, social justice, and personal responsibility as we "create action-oriented, learning-focused communities in schools" (Pajak, p. 292). Both Osborn and Pajak believe that liberal-democratic values must be shared and taught in North American society while allowing and encouraging a diversity of cultures. Democracy is a North American value that must be maintained as educators explore the changing requirements of a new global reality in our world (Osborn, 1999; Pajak, 2000).

In separate texts, Osborn and Pajak address the increased challenges that are created by mounting cultural diversities in North American public schools. It has been suggested that, "given the present fragmentation of civil society under the pressures of increasing diversity" (Sergiovanni, 2002, p. 50), the purpose of education and schooling should be reevaluated for we now live in a technologically advanced, global society that imposes nontraditional demands upon its citizens. Educators are now expected to produce students who are capable of succeeding in this new international culture. As a result, there are fundamental changes occurring in education both internationally and nationally in the 21st century. The traditional, cultural view of education has shifted to include:

All students can and will learn at higher levels than in the past.

The school will rally around the goal of higher achievement for all students.

Schools will be restructured to focus on improving the quality of student learning.

As a consequence, alternative models of education should be evaluated thoroughly as part of this evident need for school restructuring. As we address various rallying points for change, we must exercise caution to ensure that our decisions are in the best interest of student learning (Osborn, 1999; Pajak, 2000; Sergiovanni, 2002).

At first glance, it appears that the International Baccalaureate does indeed satisfy Pajak's economic rallying point for change. However, two factors come to mind when contemplating the implementation of an International Baccalaureate Programme. The first factor reports back to the International Baccalaureate's original propose as an option for highly capable, internationally mobile students who are university bound. In regards to this first factor, the International Baccalaureate programme "is regarded as a credential for admission to the most selective universities all over the world" (Tookey, 1999, p. 3). The International Baccalaureate Organization has been very successful in the creation of an internationally excepted programme of study that qualifies highly motivated university bound students for entry into leading universities. The programme maintains high international standards, creates a strong academic atmosphere, rewards diverse abilities and talents, provides challenges for students, and motivates highly capable students. Schools considering International Baccalaureate Programmes would be wise to reflect on the potential benefits to gifted and talented students. There is ample evidence to imply that the culture of a successfully implemented International Baccalaureate Programme is beneficial to the continued growth of gifted and talented students. When viewed through a conservative lens, the programme meets the academic, cognitive, motivational, emotional, and social needs of exceptional students (Paris, 2003; Poelzer, 1997; Tookey, 1999).

Pajak's second point for change revolves around social justice, public responsibility, multicultural and gender issues, and the environment. This much more liberal second area of concern is primarily associated with the issue of homogenization and globalization of society. Essentially, cultures that implement an International Baccalaureate Programme potentially relinquish local values and practices of education to those deemed valuable to the world. From this point of view, the International Baccalaureate Programmes are "very much a process of globalization rather than a process of internationalism" (Paris, p. 235). There is a potential loss of local control for school districts considering an International Baccalaureate Programme. Globalization occurs "when there are impositions of ideas involving a dominant-recessive relationship (Paris, 2003). Internationalization on the other hand occurs "when there is a sharing of ideas, where ideas are utilized, agreed upon, and mutually accepted" (Paris, 2003). The issue for schools considering International Baccalaureate Programmes involves questions about how much local control is acceptable to relinquish. Are districts sharing the ideas of educators internationally or simply implementing a pre-described programme that fundamentally changes or ignores local values in education? Are districts entering into recessive positions and allowing an external organization to dominate or control? This study can not answer these questions for individual schools and districts considering the implementation of an International Baccalaureate Programme, I can simply bring this component of the decision making process to the attention of decision makers.

A Comparison of the International Baccalaureate with Other Programmes

The International Baccalaureate Programme and the Advanced Placement Programme are designed to meet the educational needs of high school students who are motivated and prepared for academic challenges beyond those that characterize most high school curricula. Since they are the only two nationally recognized, comprehensive, and multi-subject programmes offered for this purpose in the United States and Canada, it seems natural to start my comparison with the Advanced Placement (AP) Programme. I have discussed the International Baccalaureate Programme above. However, in order to better compare the two educational programmes, it is necessary to give a brief outline of the Advanced Placement Programme.

In 1953, the American College Board began the Advanced Placement Programme to challenge a small, elite group of able students. Advanced Placement students took a college course in high school and an external exam to qualify for admission to advanced undergraduate work in a university or college. The strength of Advanced Placement was its eschewing fads for a solid collaboration between high school teachers and college professors, with an emphasis on subject content. An important feature was the evaluation of a high school student's work by outside examiners who were college faculty (College Board, 2004).

Since its induction in 1953, the programme has spread widely throughout North American high schools. The number of participants has more than doubled every decade. Today, more than half of American high schools and a third of four-year college-bound seniors participate in this Programme. More than a million Advanced Placement exams, five hundred times the original number, are taken each year (Lichten, 2000). Approximately 3,000 North

American universities recognize Advanced Placement courses and examinations. Students presenting qualifying grades on Advanced Placement Exams may earn anywhere from 3 to 6 credits (for a single course) to one year of college credit, and on occasion, two years of credit, thereby earning second-year and sometimes third-year standing. However, universities in North America and abroad differ regarding the exact nature of their acceptance policies.

When Harlan P. Hanson, director of the Advanced Placement Programme and a founder and member of International Baccalaureate North America, compared AP with IB with respect to rigor and acceptance of courses by universities and colleges, he pointed out that one difference between AP and IB is reflected in their aims: whereas Advanced Placement prepares students for college work in North America, the International Baccalaureate prepares students for an international range of universities. Also, though the International Baccalaureate is more international than Advanced Placement in its treatment of history and language, both programmes offer similar courses in math and science. Furthermore, a difference appears in the philosophical approaches: the International Baccalaureate prescribes structure for all, whereas Advanced Placement believes that the school should decide what the student ought to learn (Freeman, 1987).

Despite the differences between AP and IB, the College Board and the International Baccalaureate Organization feel that they also have many similarities. In a pamphlet that they co-authored, the two groups pointed out the following similarities: both are rigorous programmes devoted to educational excellence; each programme sets high performance standards for students and faculty; both programmes involve dedicated and creative teachers committed to their students, their disciplines, and their profession; both programmes attract highly motivated students who wish to excel academically and attend the most selective colleges and universities; and both programmes have attracted the attention of international educators, educational policymakers, and the general public as ways to improve the quality of education around the world (IBO and the College Board, 2002).

The International Baccalaureate Programme has also been compared with some smaller and lesser-known educational programmes. The programme is considered to be more of a well-rounded experience than those offered at special schools such as the North Carolina School of Science and Mathematics (NCSSM). Whereas the programme offered by the North Carolina School of Science and Mathematics emphasizes math and science, the International Baccalaureate Programme emphasizes no particular subjects. However, the quality of the courses in both programmes is high; NCSSM offers courses that include Advanced Placement material so that students can, if they so desire, take the Advanced Placement examinations (Eilber & Warshaw, 1988).

The International Baccalaureate Programme contrasts sharply with programmes that emphasize acceleration such as the Study of Mathematically Precocious Youth (SMPY), a programme initiated by Julian Stanley at Johns Hopkins University in the early seventies. SMPY led to talent searches that identified able learners at the age of 12 who are then given an accelerated programme in advanced mathematics. As a consequence, these able learners can take math college courses at a much earlier age (Daniel & Cox, 1985; Stanley & Benbow, 1982). Once again, though, the International Baccalaureate approach stresses balance in education between literary and scientific disciplines in order to keep all options open for as long as possible (Renaud, 1974).

There has been little research incorporating quantitative data done to compare achievement levels between International Baccalaureate students and students in other programmes. Poelzer & Feldhusen (1996) compared the achievement of biology, physics, and chemistry students in Higher Level International Baccalaureate Programmes, Subsidiary Level International Baccalaureate Programmes, and regular Alberta Programmes. In all three sciences, the International Baccalaureate students scored higher than regular students.

A more recent report, *Learning and Understanding: Improving Advanced Study of Mathematics and Science in U.S. High Schools*, was not as kind to the International Baccalaureate Programme. It sought to explore the current status of high school mathematics and science education by means of an in-depth look at Programmes designed for advanced students, such as the AP and the International Baccalaureate Programmes (Gollub, Bertenthal, Labov, Curtis, 2002). The review panel concluded that "the kinds and levels of questions that appear on both the Advanced Placement and the International Baccalaureate examinations reinforce[s] the emphasis on broad but shallow coverage of topics" (National Research Council, 2002 p.17). The National Research Council went on to say that given the emphasis on passing end-of-course exams, teachers tend to make the coursework a test-preparation seminar rather than a focus on substantive knowledge in the core content area. The council report stated that there was too much material for the high school student, thus making the learning shallow. In response, the International Baccalaureate Organization felt that not all of the criticisms were warranted since 25% of the final grades in their courses are based on laboratory notebooks, not just the final exam (Criticisms, 2002).

One of the largest studies to take a quantitative approach was done by the International Baccalaureate Organization itself. The North American Regional International Baccalaureate office (IBNA) asked all United States-based seniors pursuing either the International

Baccalaureate Diploma or the International Baccalaureate Certificates to complete the *May 2003 IBNA Voluntary Data Form* during the May 2003 exam session (International Baccalaureate Organization, 2004). In order to gather quantitative information, the IBNA surveyed 6,392 graduating International Baccalaureate seniors to find out how they had fared on national standardized tests.

In all of the measures that were included in the International Baccalaureate Organization's survey, International Baccalaureate students outperformed the general population. International Baccalaureate respondents obtained a mean Scholastic Assessment Test (SAT) score of 1274, considerably higher than the average score of 1026 of the total SAT test-taking population. Additionally, the Diploma candidates' average score was 1300, considerably higher than the average 1220 obtained by Certificate candidates. What the IBNA failed to include in their report, though, was any mention of sampling errors. Did all of the graduating International Baccalaureate students complete the survey? Was the sample population representative of the entire population?

Although a smaller group of International Baccalaureate students participated in the American College Test (ACT), International Baccalaureate students still managed to obtain a mean score of 27.1, again higher than the total test-taking average of 20.8. Once again, Diploma candidates outscored Certificate candidates by a mean score of 27.8 to 25.3.

Several respondents indicated that they had received recognition from the National merit, National Achievement, and/or National Hispanic Scholars programmes. Nine hundred seventy one International Baccalaureate students received recognition from the National Merit Programme. Most of the students recognized (86%) were Diploma Candidates. Of the total respondents recognized, 40.5% went on to become Semi-

Finalists or Finalists. In addition, 154 were recognized as National Achievement Scholars. Most of the respondents recognized (76.4%) were Diploma candidates, and of the total respondents recognized, 50% went on to become Semi-Finalists or Finalists. Lastly, 54 candidates indicated that they had received recognition from the National Hispanic Scholar programme. Of those indicating recognition, 84.6% were Diploma candidates. In addition, of the total respondents indicating recognition, 86% were recognized as Semi-Finalists or Finalists.

Do International Baccalaureate students outperform other students? Clearly, there is not an abundance of work that would allow for this question to be definitively answered. Any studies that have been undertaken concentrate on the Diploma Programme: datum focusing on the Middle Years and Primary Years Programmes is rather non-existent. The data collected by the International Baccalaureate Organization would lead one to believe that International Baccalaureate Organization students by far score higher on standardized tests than the general population. How, though, were the International Baccalaureate students chosen in the first place? Might test scores and grade point averages have played a part? This information is glaringly absent from the study. So, although the International Baccalaureate Organization's study is one of the largest and seemingly comprehensive quantitative studies to date, it is certainly one of the most suspect, given the source. Unbiased work that takes background factors like admission requirements into consideration is needed. Only then can a true comparison of achievement results between International Baccalaureate students and the general population at all grade levels be made.

University and College Recognition

It is widely recognized that participation in a rigorous high school curriculum, like that of the International Baccalaureate Diploma Programme, is one of the best predictors of whether a student will graduate from college (U.S. Department of Education, 1999). For many years, colleges and universities throughout the world have demonstrated understanding of the educational value of the International Baccalaureate Diploma Programme by recognizing it as a high school leaving certificate that effectively prepares students for post-secondary education. Thus, the International Baccalaureate has largely succeeded in its goal to be a universally recognized admissions credential. The International Baccalaureate has moved beyond its original goal of standardizing curriculum for mobile students; instead, it has grown into what has been called the "Cadillac of the College Prep Programmes" (Gehring, 2001).

Specific agreements are in place with ministries of education and universities in 102 countries that recognize the International Baccalaureate Diploma as a valid means of earning entry to postsecondary study. The International Baccalaureate Diploma is increasingly being viewed as a strong indicator of academic promise and achievement. International Baccalaureate students often have an advantage in the admissions process at selective universities. In addition, International Baccalaureate courses and exams are recognized for the purpose of advanced credit and/or placement at over 900 North American colleges and universities. In fact, over 100 postsecondary institutions now grant a full year of credit to students who have earned the International Baccalaureate Diploma (IBO, 2003).

The North American Regional International Baccalaureate office asked all United States-based

International Baccalaureate seniors to complete the *May 2003 IBNA Voluntary Data Form* during the May 2003 exam session. The survey of 6,392 International Baccalaureate seniors who graduated in 2003 showed that International Baccalaureate students in the USA are getting admitted to university at higher rates than their peers. College-admissions officers at many schools say, "IB [has] acquired the status of [a] backstage pass at a rock concert" (Matthews, 2003). 98.5% of the respondents indicated that they had applied for post-secondary admission and 97% indicated that they had been accepted. In addition, 22.9% indicated that they had received early admission to a university or college (International Baccalaureate Organization, 2004).

Additionally, the survey asked students to report where they were admitted and from which schools they were turned down. International Baccalaureate North America then compared the acceptance rate for these International Baccalaureate students to the overall acceptance rate published by individual colleges and universities (IBO, 2004). All respondents tended to be granted acceptance at a higher rate than the total population, and International Baccalaureate Diploma candidates were granted admission at a much higher rate than the total population (See Table 3.1).

Table 3.1

University Acceptance Rates for Incoming Freshmen Fall 2004

INSTITU-TION	ALL APPLICANTS	ALL IB APPLICANTS	DIPLOMA CANDIDATE APPLICANTS
University of Florida	58.0%	88.4%	88.9%
Virginia Polytechnic Institute	66.0%	67.9%	80.2%
James Madison University	58.0%	65.1%	76.9%
University of Virginia	39.0%	55.9%	61.3%
University of California, Los Angeles	24.0%	41.1%	48.5%
University of California, San Diego	41.0%	60.5%	65.5%
University of California, Berkeley	24.0%	45.4%	50.6%
Florida State University	70.0%	92.9%	94.6%
George Mason University	66.0%	88.4%	97.5%
University of California, Irvine	56.0%	85.5%	89.9%
College of William and Mary	35.0%	49.3%	53.9%
Harvard University	11.0%	12.5%	**12.1%**
Duke University	25.0%	36.2%	**39.4%**
Stanford University	13.0%	16.8%	**17.6%**
New York University	33.0%	47.0%	**52.8%**
University of Central	62.0%	95.7%	**95.9%**

Florida			
University of North Carolina, Chapel Hill	35.0%	57.8%	**63.6%**
Yale University	13.0%	14.3%	**15.1%**
University of California, Santa Barbara	51.0%	69.2%	**74.8%**
University of Southern California	30.0%	69.0%	**76.7%**
Column Average	**40.5%**	**58.1%**	**62.8%**

Note: Only universities with more than 20 total IB applicants are included. The acceptance rates for "all applicants" were provided by each respective institution

International Baccalaureate students appear to fare very well. Of the 170 universities that received more than 20 applications from International Baccalaureate students, only one had a lower admission rate for International Baccalaureate students than for the overall applicant pool. Quite often, the International Baccalaureate acceptance rate was double or triple the overall rate. At 29 of the 170 universities with 20 or more International Baccalaureate applicants, 100% of the International Baccalaureate students were admitted. However, upon closer examination of the study, questions arise. Why would not all of the universities and their corresponding acceptance rates be included in the table? Also, wouldn't the inclusion of averages and ranges provide credibility to the table? Additionally, is it not a logical conclusion that Diploma candidates would be accepted at a higher rate than other International Baccalaureate students? The datum becomes suspect when points such as these come to light.

University recognition is obviously a major concern

for International Baccalaureate students, parents and counselors. In fact, of all the students worldwide who graduate with International Baccalaureate credentials, well over half of them matriculate to post-secondary institutions in Canada or the USA (IBO, 2004). Therefore, it is not surprising that many North American colleges and universities have developed policies that recognize International Baccalaureate graduates. These institutions make it apparent that they understand and appreciate the International Baccalaureate student and the International Baccalaureate Diploma Programme. They do this in a number of ways: state that the International Baccalaureate Diploma is taken into account in the admissions process; provide a full year of credit for students who earn the International Baccalaureate Diploma; recognize standard level courses and exams by providing credit and/or placement for standard level results; recognize Theory of Knowledge; recognize the Extended Essay; provide detailed information on the college courses for which students can receive credit based on their International Baccalaureate exam scores; and provide scholarships or scholarship opportunities specifically for International Baccalaureate students (IBO, 2003). Many North American colleges and universities recognize International Baccalaureate graduates. However, the International Baccalaureate Organization fails to mention how these students rank amongst all other students entering these post-secondary institutions. Perhaps they are the highest ranked applicants and deserve special notice. If this is the case, the recognition is not due solely to the International Baccalaureate status like the International Baccalaureate Organization would like the readers of their website to believe.

The University of Alberta, the recipient of more International Baccalaureate transcripts than any other university in Canada, recognizes the academic background of students enrolled in the International Baccalaureate Diploma Programme. Admission for International Baccalaureate students is based on the higher of either the high school grade or the International Baccalaureate score. A grade conversion scale has been implemented for this purpose. The University of Alberta grants advance credit or advanced placement in a number of International Baccalaureate courses (Higher and Standard Levels) with scores of 6 or 7. The extent to which advance standing is granted varies upon the degree programme to which the student is admitted. Students who are granted the International Baccalaureate Diploma, and obtain a combined score of zero or better on the Extended Essay and the Theory of Knowledge component, are granted advance credit for a 3-credit Junior Open Elective. Each year, fifty International Baccalaureate Diploma Scholarships are awarded on the basis of academic achievement to International Baccalaureate Diploma graduates who register at the University of Alberta (University of Alberta, 2004).

Also interesting to examine is the University of British Columbia's policy towards International Baccalaureate students. With over 600 applicants from the International Baccalaureate in 2003, it was the third highest recipient of International Baccalaureate students in North America. They are also among the most generous universities worldwide when granting first-year credit for International Baccalaureate courses. For example, UBC will grant 6 credits of philosophy for scores of A or B on Theory of Knowledge. Scores of 5 or 6 on higher-level International Baccalaureate courses will typically result in first year credit at UBC. International Baccalaureate students have flexibility when applying the first-year credit they are granted. Students have the option of either accepting the credit or repeating the credited course (University of British Columbia, 2004).

The University of British Columbia (UBC) thinks that International Baccalaureate students become outstanding university students; their scholarships awarded reflect this. Of all the International Baccalaureate students from Canada admitted to UBC in 2004, 46% received a scholarship. Students who had an anticipated score of 35 or a final score of 32 (including bonus points) were automatically awarded the Undergraduate Scholars Programme, a complete scholarship package that included $2,500, early registration and a guaranteed place in UBC residence (University of British Columbia, 2004).

UBC also feels that the combination of critical thinking, research and writing skills learned in the International Baccalaureate Programme enables students to succeed in the university learning environment. Because of the skills they have learned, International Baccalaureate students provide leadership in classroom discussion and group learning. Figures reflect this claim: International Baccalaureate students who registered directly into second year courses scored an average of 7% to 12% higher than their classmates. By taking the International Baccalaureate philosophy to its next logical progression, UBC fosters the success of International Baccalaureate students and challenges them to take their skills to the international stage (University of British Columbia, 2004).

The academic rigor of the International Baccalaureate Programme also seems to be borne out by other authors such as Daniel & Cox (1992) and Thomas, (1998), whose research found that in forty universities across the United States, International Baccalaureate graduates have higher grade point averages than the average college entrant. Similarly, Peterson (1987) found that college students who had International Baccalaureate credentials performed better as undergraduates than did those without International Baccalaureate credentials. Also, in 1994, McGill University conducted a study of

International Baccalaureate graduates and found that they performed better academically than non- International Baccalaureate students (Schofield, 1999). The information presented in these research studies does seem interesting but, once again, must be taken in context. For example, how were the International Baccalaureate students initially granted admission into the Programme? If a high level of motivation was an original factor, it seems only natural that this drive would continue into the university years. Although additional research is needed, the literature does seem to indicate that participants in the International Baccalaureate Diploma Programme perform quite well on standardized tests, are accepted into colleges and universities at high rates, and frequently receive national recognition for their academic performance. However, it is important to note that many schools have instituted criteria for admission into the International Baccalaureate Programme at their school. Test scores, grade point averages and teacher recommendations are just a few of the possible factors considered for admission into some International Baccalaureate Programmes. This result indicates that some students are accepted into the programme because they are intelligent and highly motivated. Would they not fair quite well, regardless of educational programme? This should be taken into account when comparing International Baccalaureate students to the overall population. Correlation of International Baccalaureate students and test scores or university acceptance rates does not, necessarily, demonstrate causation. Additionally, what is noticeably absent from the literature is research geared at the Middle Years Programme and Primary Years Programme. Also unfortunate is the concentration of studies based in the United States. Little work has been done within Canada to evaluate the International Baccalaureate Programme against Canadian national standards. So, while the research seems to indicate that the International Baccalaureate Diploma Programme provides quality curriculum to students, further research in this area would no doubt be illuminating. However, the academic lens is only one perspective from which to evaluate the International Baccalaureate Programme. Economic, political, cultural and physical lenses must also be considered.

An Economic Perspective

The economics of choice

The North Vancouver School District (NVSD) has projected an operating budget shortfall of $7.5M for the next three years. A major part of this deficit resulted in a grant reduction of $2M due to lower enrollment. Consequently, one of the North Vancouver School District revenue options is to keep its current student base and attract new students from outside of North Vancouver. This option speaks to the increasing competition, in large part due to open enrollment, for school survival and is directly linked to providing greater choice for parents and students. Open enrollment is defined as giving parents the ability to choose a school despite neighborhood boundaries. Educators, such as "principal Neil Wyatt at Colonel By Secondary School in Ottawa credits the introduction of the International Baccalaureate programme with helping to ensure the school's survival: more than half its students come from outside its official catchment area" (Schofield, 1999, p.92). In this context, the International Baccalaureate Primary Years Programme (PYP), Middle Years Programme (MYP) and Diploma Programme (IBDP) provides the financial and academic means to attract new and current students within a climate of greater parental school choice.

Under British Columbia's new open enrollment

policy, Brown (2004) compiled the results of numerous parent interviews regarding school choice. Academic achievement and student discipline ranked among the highest reasons for school selection (Brown, 2004). Additionally, Smedley (1995) and Raptis and Fleming (2003) also found that parents rate high standards and discipline very highly. School choice is a major decision that can have a tremendous effect on a child's future. To that extent, a closer look at what the International Baccalaureate Programme has to offer is required prior to implementation.

While the literature appears to support the International Baccalaureate Programme's claim to increase student international understanding, the term "international understanding" can be difficult to define. Hinrichs (2003), in his study comparing the levels of international understanding among International Baccalaureate and Advanced Placement students, compiled categories of international understanding from authors that use similar descriptions in their research (table 2.2). He attempted to identify if students increase their international understanding as a result of participating in the International Baccalaureate Diploma Program.

The International Understanding Survey Questionnaire was administered to 27 junior and 26 senior International Baccalaureate students, and to 28 junior and 22 senior Advanced Placement (AP) English and/or Social Studies students (Hinrichs, 2003). The student population came from a high school in a school near Seattle, Washington. Students also wrote their personal definitions of international understanding. Although, International Baccalaureate Diploma Programme and Advanced Placement students did not differ significantly on any of the categories of the survey questionnaire, the International Baccalaureate Diploma Program students scored significantly higher in terms of their personal definitions.

The numbers in Table 3.2 represent the presence of these seven international understanding categories within each student's definition. The table further illustrates a noticeable difference between International Baccalaureate Diploma Program and Advanced Placement students. However, the author astutely points out "the number of students in the study was small and the results could not be generalized to a wider population or a population outside this geographic area" (Hinrichs, 2003, p.344). Still, the study does promote further interest at researching the International Baccalaureate Programme's ability to increase international understanding.

Table 3.2

Categories of international understanding

Categories	IB (N = 53)		AP (N = 50)	
	n	%	n	%
Developing personal knowledge, communication skills, attitudes, ethical reasoning, and/or responsibility necessary to live effectively across cultures.	29	55	1	2
Recognition and appreciation of ethnic diversity, cultural pluralism, and diverse values and beliefs.	46	87	24	48
Recognition of interdependence and connections of cultures and nations.	25	47	8	16
Understanding of contemporary and historical global issues, their causes and effects.	23	43	27	54
Valuing peace and international interests over nationalism and cultural identity.	4	7	1	2
Understanding how domestic policies affect the world.	10	19	6	12
Respect for democracy and for basic human rights.	5	9	2	4

Taken from Hinrichs (2003, p.340)

Such evidence can give parents and schools added insight at choosing or offering International Baccalaureate Programmes. Ultimately, "the IB programme nurtures attributes increasingly in demand in the world at large: communication skills, critical thinking and the ability to speak a second language" (Schofield, 1999, p.92). Consequently, the number of International Baccalaureate

Programmes in North America is rising. The two largest International Baccalaureate countries are the United States (406 IB schools) and Canada (89 IB schools). In 2003, as compared to last year, Canada had 5 percent more schools offering International Baccalaureate exams; 5 percent more students sitting for one or more International Baccalaureate exams; 10 percent more exams being taken, and 16 percent more International Baccalaureate Diplomas being awarded (Sjogren & Campbell, 2003, p.55). It seems parents and school districts are making a choice.

In terms of schools and school districts choosing to implement an International Baccalaureate Programme, it is still doubtful that the perceived high academic standard is the main reason to undertake such a programme.

When people have to pay for education, they are more likely to make investment decisions which will realize an economic return. Educational choices which best advantage their children – possibly those they feel can help their children more securely gain an advantage, particularly in the global competition for credentials – are likely to be made (Potter & Hayden, 2004, p.91).

The same standard may apply for schools and school districts. For instance, is the introduction of an International Baccalaureate Programme equated only to economic survival masked as an educational opportunity? A closer analysis of the costs will be required before attaining an answer.

Cost Analysis of the International Baccalaureate Programme

Before an International Baccalaureate Programme can be implemented, schools and school districts will need to conduct a feasibility study identifying resources and enter what International Baccalaureate North America (IBNA, 2004) terms the consideration or investigation phase. This first of three phases involves: sending staff and administrators to workshops, gaining support from the school community, developing an implementation plan, purchasing International Baccalaureate related publications, and initial curriculum development. The second phase involves candidate schools consolidating planning and implementation details. The final phase comprises the review of the applicant school and authorization or rejection to become an International Baccalaureate school (Prospective Schools Information, 2004).

The details within each phase vary depending on the level of the programme. Table 3.3 summarizes the 2004-2005 fee structure in Canadian dollars unless stated otherwise stated.

Table 3.3

International Baccalaureate Fees for Schools

Prospective Schools / Candidate Schools	

Application Part A (Intent to Apply) *
This sum must accompany a school's request to become a candidate school. It covers all costs for
    Two day consultation visit by mentor
    Services of a consultant for one academic year
Subscription to the Online Curriculum Centre for one year
	$6400

Application Part B This sum must accompany a school's request for authorization. It covers all costs of reading application and a two day authorization visit.	**$6700**

Annual Basic Fee
This fee is payable by authorized schools and is due 1 September of each academic year. It includes:
    Copies of all newly developed curriculum and teacher support guides
    Subscription to *IB World* Magazine
Subscription to Online Curriculum Centre
	$3100 USD PYP, MYP
	
	$8180 USD DP

Programme Evaluation Fee This fee is charged 3-5 years after authorization. It covers all costs for a two day visit.	**$4500**

Other costs – budgeted by the school
    Ongoing teacher training at IB workshops
    Time to plan for application
    IB publications for teachers
    Costs for the PYP, MYP, DP Coordinators
        (min. 25% release time)
Resources for second language teaching and internationalism
	$660 each

* In Part A, Diploma Programme Prospective Schools have the option to not request a mentor making the fee only $1500.
Taken from the PYP, MYP and IBDP Prospective Schools Information, IBNA August 2004

Clearly with the costs outlined in this table, school districts have to make a value assessment. Are the costs worth it? According to one author, the suggestion is "if you build it, they will come" (Hargrove, 2003). Consequently, politicians are taking note and in Florida additional funding and scholarship funds are given for successful International Baccalaureate final exam completion (Schofield, 1999). However, given the high costs to start up and maintain an International Baccalaureate programme at any level, a great deal of consideration needs to be given to the finances prior to implementation.

Again the question arises, is best practice or economic survival dictating the rationale to implement an International Baccalaureate Programme? If the answer is the former, Codrington "argues that best practice in international schools should focus...to meet the individual needs of each student, including ongoing professional development and feedback for teachers, and emphasizes a clear separation of governance and management" (2004, p. 173). However, the reality seems to show that benefits and costs are considered articulated together.

The 'business approach' to education can be characterized with a "focus on control, accountability and achievement of short term goals" (Codrington, 2004, p.177). Central to this discussion is the meaning of accountability. Robertson (2003) outlines two different interpretations:

> One represents accountability as giving an account of one's practices voluntarily, the other as being called to account by another party; the former is an internal form of accountability emphasizing trust and support, the latter is an external form of accountability emphasizing pressure and inspection (p.277).

It is this second interpretation that describes a

market-based accountability. Hence, what are the teachers' perceptions of accountability at an international school? Which interpretation does the International Baccalaureate Organization advocate? What forms of accountability measures are enforced in an International Baccalaureate school? Poulson (1998) identifies four forms of accountability to:

oneself and one's values – moral accountability
other professionals or colleagues within an occupation
  or institution – professional accountability
clients or stakeholders of the institution – client
  accountability
funders, government – contractual accountability

It is the client accountability that has recently defined educational accountability in British Columbia. Unfortunately, this type of accountability has been externally imposed, thereby hegemonic in nature. "The neo-liberal economic hegemonic consensus brought about by the predominantly New Right governments in many Anglophone countries over the last 20 years have been the driving force for such a free-market, business approach to educational accountability" (Robertson, 2003, p.281). The free-market aspect represents client accountability in an environment where educators must be accountable to its stakeholders. Hence, a client accountability emerged that was externally imposed on education with the assumption that the use of business strategies would be the best method to reform education. This equates to an emphasis on quantitative measures.

Quantitative measures translate into standardized testing for measuring student achievement. These fixed performance indicators allow school based competition to thrive by:

...allowing school choice by opening boundaries within and across school systems, school privatization plans, the creation of charter schools, magnet schools, academies and other specialized educational facilities. Competition also is increased by altering the basis for school funding so that money follows students (e.g. vouchers, tuition tax credits), and publicly ranking schools based on aggregated student achievement scores. These tools are often used in combination (Leithwood et al., 1999, p.21-2).

The adoption of a market approach to evaluate education is synonymous with the client version. The question remains, is this external approach that seems to foster greater client accountability, improving our educational systems? Several studies have shown that this free-market approach has actually had an opposite effect (Macpherson et al., 1997, Ball et al., 1997). For instance, the trend toward decentralizing schools in order to become more competitive has actually led to increased centralization and resulted in less, not more public involvement. Consequently, it has produced a hierarchy of schools with "schools selecting parents rather than parents selecting schools" (Macpherson et al., 1997, p.7). Are programmes like the International Baccalaureate affected by this neo-liberal economic hegemony?

The International Baccalaureate Organization does use external accountability measures for schools wanting to run their programmes. For instance, the schools are visited prior to becoming an authorized International Baccalaureate school to ensure specific requirements have been met. After authorization, a school will be monitored through evaluation visits. In terms of teacher and student accountability, there are measures required to ensure the successful implementation of the programme. These include teacher workshops and an importance on criterion-based evaluation. Unlike the Primary Years and Middle Years Programmes, the International Baccalaureate

Diploma Programme "is largely based on external examinations, which provides a certain degree of standardization intended to enable universities to assess students' level of achievement" (Robertson, 2003, p.294). Robertson's study (2003) found that these external measures were generally well supported by all stakeholders. It was also reported that despite these external accountability measures, the school still emphasized professional accountability and flexibility that countered any hegemonic sentiments. When compared to other schools, the international school did not seem to be adversely affected by neo-liberal economic hegemony (Robertson, 2003).

Clearly, economic survival in an increasing climate of competition must be considered when evaluating the implementation of an International Baccalaureate programme. Yet does this consideration override all academic considerations and any notion of 'best practice.' Within these considerations comes the question of accountability. This term has taken a hegemonic meaning in the educational world and needs to be further investigated as it relates to an International Baccalaureate Programme.

A Political Perspective

The politics of school choice

What are the political issues surrounding school choice? After reviewing various publications, legislation, policies and research, the first issue appears to be with the term itself. What exactly is school choice? The term is used in a wide variety of ways that might be best thought of in terms of four basic clusters along a continuum (Richmond School District, 2001; Smith and Kleine, 1995).

A brief explanation of each of these clusters is needed in order to clarify what "choice" means in reference to the International Baccalaureate Programme. At one end of the continuum is personal control. This refers to programmes in which parents or students have more control over the educational experience than in typical cases. Parents might be able to choose a child's teacher or determine curriculum objectives, learning materials, instructional strategies or assessment techniques. Students also may be permitted to choose some of their courses. In some cases, school choice refers to alternate programmes. These programmes operate at the school or district level, and are based on individual preference (elective courses in secondary schools, school based enrichment programmes, and specialty programmes) or are based on an objectively identified learning need (district learning support services). Sometimes, alternate programmes are proposed as options within a school and sometimes as the focus of an entire school, in which the term "magnet school" is sometimes used. Moving further along the continuum of school choice is the concept of open boundaries. Open boundaries refer to instances in which parents/students choose to attend schools outside their catchment area or designated/neighborhood school. At the opposite end of the choice continuum is vouchers. Vouchers refer to funding which comes directly from the state/province for parents/students to use to register or enroll their children in public or private schools of their choice (Brayne, 2004; Richmond School District, 2001).

The continuum described above is useful in helping to clarify what "choice" refers to. It is a convenient way of grouping programmes into specific clusters; however, in doing so the continuum is also problematic. In many instances, programmes do not fit neatly into one specific cluster, and may have components of one or more clusters and as such are not able to be easily classified as "parental control" or "alternate programme"; "alternate programme" or "open boundary". This is the case with the International Baccalaureate Programme. International Baccalaureate Programmes fall under the heading of alternate programmes, as they are programmes specifically designed to meet individual students' learning needs, and in doing so offer students' specialty courses and programming. They also fall into the category of open boundaries, as they are offered only at specific schools and not at every neighborhood school.

The issue of school choice is a contentious one, with advocates and opponents of school choice each having strong and valid reasons for their particular views and opinions. Individuals who advocate for school choice each have their own specific reasons, but based on the research (Brayne, 2004: Ryan and Heise, 2002; Richmond School District, 2001; Hill, 1996; Viteretti, 1996) there appears to be two clear categories of motivation, individual liberty and market forces.

Those who advocate for school choice on the basis of individual liberty have a strong aversion to the monopoly of the public school system and the restrictions imposed on personal choice by the government. They believe that choice in schools and programmes will cause a higher level of parent support and involvement, and in doing so will improve student learning. The International Baccalaureate Programme clearly is a programme in which there is strong parental involvement and a strong academic/learning focus (IBO, 2004).

The second category has a more direct focus on improving student learning through competition and market forces. This is based on the belief that the same dynamics that drive an open economy can be applied to education.

The freedom of individuals to choose their programme or school is fundamental to this approach. Advocates claim that market forces result in increased creativity and productivity by requiring programmes and schools to improve; weeding out ineffective programmes and schools; and expanding successful programmes and schools. The International Baccalaureate programme is a specialized programme, which is based on a common philosophy and common characteristics. The programme aims to develop the whole student, and helps students to grow intellectually, socially, and culturally (IBO, 2004). The International Baccalaureate Organization (IBO) works with schools, governments and international organizations to develop challenging programmes of international education and rigorous assessment. This structure ensures that the International Baccalaureate Programme is evaluated frequently, and adapted in order to meet the current demands of the market.

Opponents of school choice argue that expertise and social cohesion are two issues of concern (Richmond School District, 2001). They hold that public education is a complex affair and that the interests of children and community are best served by allowing experts to determine educational objectives, student needs, and the most effective programmes to meet those needs. They contend that it should be a professional assessment of needs that should determine a student's basic educational programme, not the personal choice of parents or the student. These concerns are certainly upheld when discussing a programme like the International Baccalaureate. The second issue surrounds social cohesion. Social cohesion is only created when all elements of society meet, share common experiences, and learn to live with and respect each other, thus establishing norms of inclusiveness and reciprocity. The purpose of public schools in a democratic society is to offer schools and programmes that reinforce these norms. This purpose, however, is undermined when the system is fragmented by a range of schools and different programmes, such as the International Baccalaureate Programme.

School choice is wrought with political issues, including: the definition of the term choice, the difficulty of categorizing and classifying specific educational programmes, and the various advantages and disadvantages of choice programmes. There will always be groups in favor of the implementation of choice programmes as well as groups opposed to school choice and the implementation of choice programmes.

Admission Requirements

Each school offering an International Baccalaureate Programme is responsible for establishing its own admission requirements. As such, there are tremendous variations in admission requirements. In the Lower Mainland of British Columbia, there are many schools offering the International Baccalaureate Diploma Programme. Of the schools currently offering the International Baccalaureate Diploma Programme, there is a clear difference in admissions requirements between private and publicly funded schools. There are also differences in admissions requirements for the Primary Years Programme and the Middle Years Programme (http://www.stratfordhall.bc.ca; http://www.vsb.bc.ca). For example, Sir Winston Churchill Secondary is a publicly funded grade 8-12 high school located in Vancouver, BC. Churchill offers the International Baccalaureate Diploma Programme. Students wishing to get into the programme must write an entrance exam and submit copies of marks and current report cards. The programme is offered at no cost to students. The International Baccalaureate Diploma Programme is also offered at Britannia Secondary School in Vancouver, BC. Britannia Secondary is also a publicly funded (8-12) school; however the admission process differs from that at Churchill. At Britannia, students are admitted based on the results of testing, interviews, report cards and marks, and a handwritten essay detailing why the student wishes to be in the programme. Stratford Hall is a K -12 independent school located in Vancouver, BC. All three IB programmes (Primary Years, Middle Years and Diploma Programme) are currently offered. It is currently the only school offering the Primary Years Programme in the province of British Columbia. At Stratford Hall, students in the Primary Years Programme are characterized as: inquirers, thinkers, communicators, principled, caring and open-minded, risk-takers, knowledgeable, reflective and well-balanced (http://www.stratfordhall.bc.ca). In order to be accepted into the programme an enrollment application along with the evaluation fee of C$160.50 is required before an assessment is arranged. The first round of student assessment is in early March. Students are first assessed in small groups doing a variety of play-oriented tasks. This is followed by a one-on-one session with a teacher who will determine the child's current level of knowledge and skill. If the student is deemed to have the characteristics discussed above, they will be admitted into the PYP at Stratford Hall. The basic annual tuition for students in the Primary Years Programme is C$7700. At Stratford Hall, students interested in the Middle Years Programme and International Baccalaureate Diploma Programmes are required to demonstrate their abilities in mathematics, writing, reading comprehension, and general knowledge in a teacher-led session. In addition, previous and current report cards must be presented.

To date, the International Baccalaureate Organization has not established a common set of admission requirements for entrance into the Primary Years Programme, Middle Years Programme, or International

Baccalaureate Diploma Programme. As a result, the admissions process is left up to the discretion of the admitting school. This gives the school a significant amount of leeway in determining which students are accepted into the programme and which students are not. Are the academically bright and elite accepted more frequently? Are the multi-talented and well rounded students given an equal opportunity? The following section will address these important questions.

The Charge of Elitism in International Baccalaureate Programmes

What is meant by the term elitism? Elitism is often defined as the selection and treatment of people as superior in some way and therefore favored. This connotation creates negative feelings toward those selected (http://www.pleasantan.k12.ca.us). It has been argued that International Baccalaureate Programmes are elitist and serve only a privileged population (Ryan and Heise, 2002; Hill, 1996; Herron, 1985). Is this a valid argument?

At its inception in 1968, the International Baccalaureate Diploma Programme was generally found in private, international schools that tended to serve privileged families. Today the International Baccalaureate Organization (IBO) offers three programmes to schools: the Diploma Programme, for students in grades 11/12; the Middle Years Programme, adopted in 1994, for students ages 11 to 16; and the Primary Years Programme, adopted in 1997, for students aged 3-12. The International Baccalaureate Organization has always been committed to making an International Baccalaureate education available to students from all types of backgrounds. This is particularly true in North America where over 90% of schools offering the International Baccalaureate are public schools (IBO, 2004). These are schools of all types –urban, suburban, magnet, comprehensive, wealthy, poor and mixed socio-economic populations – and their International Baccalaureate Programmes serve all types of students.

It has also been argued that International Baccalaureate Programmes are elitist in that they primarily serve gifted and honours students (Ryan and Heise, 2002; Hill, 1996; Herron, 1985). The International Baccalaureate Organization permits International Baccalaureate authorized schools to implement their programmes in ways that will best meet their local needs. This means that there are a wide variety of student enrollment patterns in International Baccalaureate Programmes across North America. This variety is particularly apparent in the International Baccalaureate Diploma Programme. Many schools see the International Baccalaureate Diploma Programme as a way to address the needs of gifted and honours students; as a result these schools tend to have selection criteria (such as grade point average, standardized test scores, teacher recommendations, essays) for admission to their International Baccalaureate Diploma Programmes. Other schools, however, allow any willing student to attempt to enter the programme and often provide specific services to support students in their efforts.

While the International Baccalaureate Diploma Programme and occasionally the Middle Years Programme are implemented by schools as programmes for a select group of students, the Primary Years Programme is not. The Primary Years Programme is expressly designed for every student on campus, using what is referred to as "a whole-school approach." This programme focuses on the development of the whole child, addressing social, physical, emotional and cultural needs. It also gives children a strong foundation in all of the major areas of knowledge and strives to help children develop an international perspective by becoming aware and sensitive to different points of view.

As evidenced in the aforementioned section, the charge of elitism does not seem to be well grounded. Although schools are granted their own discretion in selecting students for the programme, the International Baccalaureate Organization firmly indicates that the programme is designed to meet the needs of a variety of students, not just the best and the brightest. By admitting students with various skills and talents, the IB programme encourages and caters to a wide variety of students. The fact that the programme caters to various students is important, as it ensures that there is continued interest in the International Baccalaureate Programme by many different types of students, which in turn, contributes to the sustainability of the programme.

Sustainability

In order for an International Baccalaureate programme to be sustainable, it will need to attract a given number of students. As Hill (1996) suggests in *The Educational Consequences of Choice*, it is possible for a school or programme to rely on a reputation for exclusivity or superior quality, but not all programmes can credibly claim to be the best. He suggests, however, that every school or programme can offer something that gives it an identity – a specific curriculum, social climate, or extracurricular programme – that attracts the interest of parents and students. He adds that once a school or programme has established an identity, it must deliver on its promises well enough to keep current students from transferring out of the programme, create a certain loyalty among families with several children, and attract enough new students each year.

In order to teach International Baccalaureate recognized courses, teachers must acquire the prerequisite training offered by the International Baccalaureate Organization. In North America, the International Baccalaureate Organization has recently implemented a four-tiered training model: Orientation, Level 1, Level 2 and Level 3 (IBO, 2004). Depending on one's teaching experience and more specifically, one's International Baccalaureate teaching experience, training is delivered in a workshop-based format.

The first tier is Orientation. According to the IBO (http://www.ibo.org), this is an introductory workshop that is designed for school officials and leaders investigating the feasibility of bringing an International Baccalaureate programme to their schools. Level 1 is an application & authorization workshop that provides training and assistance for schools that have decided to apply for IB authorization. Level 2 is specifically for teachers who have completed Level 1 training and/or who teach in schools that have begun to implement an International Baccalaureate Programme. Level 3 are topical seminars (three to five days in length) which cover topics of interest to both new and advanced International Baccalaureate teachers but do not necessarily prepare schools, teachers, and students for processes unique to the International Baccalaureate. Level 3 and orientation workshops are the only workshops open to teachers outside of the International Baccalaureate. The following tables (3.4 and 3.5) explain the workshops in further detail.

Table 3.4
Levels of training offered by the International Baccalaureate Organization

Teaching Experience/ Orientation	Level 1	Level 2	Level 3
New/*New*	X		
Experienced/*New*		X	X
Experienced/*Experienced*			X
All Educators	X		X

Adapted from www.ibo.org

Table 3.5
Workshop Levels/Goals/Objectives

Workshop Level	Goals
Orientation	To provide accurate information concerning IB programmes. To provide a resource for schools and school systems considering IB programmes.
Level 1	To provide accurate information to schools planning application to the IB. To increase the ease of application and authorization. To enable schools and teachers to be successful in early years of IB
Level 2	To improve the quality of authorized schools' IB programmes. To form a community of schools offering IB Programmes.
Level 3	To improve the quality of authorized schools' IB programmes. To form a community of schools offering IB Programmes.

Adapted from the International Baccalaureate Website (www.ibo.org)

The International Baccalaureate Organization offers workshops in various locations in North America throughout the year. However, the number of workshops offered in North America is minimal. North American workshops are usually only offered in major cities in Canada and the United States. It is difficult to obtain the training without having to travel considerable distances to attend workshops. In the period spanning from October 2004 – March 2005, the Level 1 workshops were only available in Charlotte, NC; Montreal, QC; Chicago, IL; Vancouver, BC; and Salt Lake City, UT (www.ibo.org). Considering the number of International Baccalaureate Programmes currently in existence in Canada and the United States, this seems quite limited. Linked to the issues of teacher professional development and training by the International Baccalaureate Organization are the issues surrounding teachers' unions.

Union Issues

Teachers' unions are an important voice in the process of school choice and International Baccalaureate implementation. Unions have played a crucial role in protecting the rights of teachers, improving working conditions in schools, and attaining more competitive salaries. Union leaders have been at the forefront of initiatives to upgrade teaching and performance standards in education. One issue that has arisen in reference to the International Baccalaureate Programme is the fact that teachers must complete the training required by the International Baccalaureate Organization in order to teach in an International Baccalaureate Programme. If, for example, a teacher without International Baccalaureate certification had more seniority than a teacher with the certification and both were vying for the same job, who does one hire? Most unions state that, all other issues being equal, the person who has seniority should get the job. The International Baccalaureate Organization, however, stipulates that the training educators must take to be International Baccalaureate certified is professional education and, as such, if the person with the most seniority applies for the job, they should be given the job provided they complete the requisite training.

A Political Summary

The Political Perspective discussed above details some of the difficult issues surrounding the implementation of an International Baccalaureate Programme. Issues arise surrounding the implementation of a programme of choice. There are also many questions surrounding the admissions process and charges of elitism regarding such programmes. In addition, there is controversy surrounding the required teacher professional development and training by the International Baccalaureate Organization. Currently there is not a lot of empirical research to support or refute these issues, nor have any definitive conclusions been made. Taken together, are these issues enough to warrant being cautious about the implementation of an International Baccalaureate Programme? Or, are they just an inevitable fact of implementing an alternative programme of choice which will always be met with opposition by some groups?

A Cultural Perspective

By nature, school culture is a qualitative lens through which to view school. It is the atmosphere present within the school that affects the quality of learning and teaching that takes place in an institution. A positive school climate opens doors, allows for risk-taking, and broadens the horizon of learning success. A controversial school climate can be frustrating, cause deception, make learning difficult, and if not addressed, lead to a negative school climate. A negative school climate is stifling. In determining the viability of an International Baccalaureate program in a school, one must carefully analyze the current school culture. Any signs of controversy must be addressed before a new program can be successfully implemented because the International Baccalaureate Programme, in and of itself will have both positive and negative effects on the overall attitudes, awareness, and achievements of students, teachers, administrators, parents, and community.

The International Baccalaureate programme is intended to meet the academic and social needs of gifted individuals. According to Tookey, author of *The International Baccalaureate*, the curriculum emphasizes "high international standards... and an atmosphere that provides tangible positive consequences for excellence... various sets of criteria for each subject, acknowledge and reward diverse abilities..." (99/2000, p. 11). Additionally, the program values diversity and challenge and provides opportunities for personal work and motivation (Tookey, 99/2000, p. 11). It is essential for the teaching staff to work effectively and strive to implement these values in their classrooms so that students will benefit academically and culturally.

The positive culture generally found in schools with International Baccalaureate Programmes is one of many desired outputs in primary, middle, and secondary schools. The strict adherence to the aforementioned standards from preliminary review through program implementation and periodic evaluation is vital to success. Prospective schools must be willing to adhere to elaborate standards which promote a whole school philosophy such standard A2 which states "the school promotes international-mindedness on the part of the adults and children in the community school" (www.ibo.org, Application for Primary Years Programme). In order to implement global standards, it is important that all members of the school community believe in the values addressed as well as the concept that all students are able to achieve. With the school adhering to these standards, the culture one experiences can be very rewarding. "Although the Primary Years Programme was originally developed for schools that taught students of many nationalities, the student profile clearly describes a kind of person that every school should seek to develop" (Singh, Oct. 2002, p.2). In many public schools this is a common standard that teachers and administrators strive for with their students. The International Baccalaureate programme, however, attempts to mandate it.

While there are three different International Baccalaureate Programmes, the literature suggests that the common goals are all very similar. Each program emphasizes diversity and growth. Developing a connection between curriculum objectives and attitudes of the students is vital to all of the International Baccalaureate Programmes. The breadth of the programme makes it stand apart from the public school curriculum. Allowing students to explore different cultures and creating international awareness are goals of the International Baccalaureate Programme that potentially have specific implications on students. When discussing the benefits of the program "credit was given to the International Baccalaureate curriculum breadth and language learning in facilitating mobility, both cultural and geographical" (Hayden, 1997, p.354). This breadth appears to encourage students to develop a greater tolerance and understanding towards all people. "Students identified no longer being able to relate to the racial prejudices of their peers as an effect of 'being international'" (Hayden, 1997, p. 355). These types of positive attitudes towards all people are contagious and promote a positive school culture through general awareness and peer support. It is important to note, however, that current studies have not delved into determining if positive peer relations are a direct result of programme or family influences. Nonetheless, parents and educators emphasizing these areas create a climate where children become more aware of their local and international surroundings. The International Baccalaureate Programme is dedicated to helping individuals become successful; these personal gains are extremely important in creating a positive overall atmosphere in school. "The culture that a successfully implemented IB programme can create in a school is conducive to the continued growth of a gifted adolescent academically and cognitively, as well as motivationally, emotionally, and socially" (Tookey, 99/2000, p.12). A school with this type of culture is likely to be successful in all areas; developing well rounded students and achieving high social and academic standards.

Achieving and maintaining high academic standards requires that the program implement a plethora of modern evaluation techniques. It is not enough to rely on standardized testing. Educators must employ a variety of clearly outlined rubrics, portfolio assessments, and traditional testing. They must also make sure that assessments are differentiated (Tookey, 2000). The variety of evaluative techniques employed by International Baccalaureate Programmes allow for more learning styles to prosper and create a more positive culture. The more success there is, the better the attitude of the people in the organization. Interestingly, some of the methods of evaluation that have been an integral part of the International Baccalaureate Programme since its inception have recently been incorporated into localized curriculums. British Columbia, for example, uses performance standards as a rubric for all teachers from kindergarten to grade 9.

While the assessment process of the International Baccalaureate Programme breeds success and establishes exceptionally high academic and social standards, it also breeds competition. Competition within schools is often attributed to promoting high achievement among the students. Unfortunately, competitive pressures can lead to immoral decision making such as cheating and sabotage. These pressures can lead to a diminished school climate. Taylor, Poegrebin, and Dodge, author's of *Advanced Placement Advanced Pressures: Academic Dishonesty Among Elite High School Students,* describe a sample of 32 students and the top 10% of their class in a Denver-based International Baccalaureate Programme. The study noted that 80% of the students had cheated to enhance their grades (December, 2002). The authors go on to say that "schools create extremely competitive environments through the process of continual testing, grading, and comparing students academically to one another" (Taylor, Poegrebin, & Dodge, 2002, p. 2). Therefore, the question of whether or not the International Baccalaureate Programme is forcing students to work beyond their capabilities arises. Additionally, Taylor, Poegrebin, and Dodge note that "accelerated students appear to perceive themselves as being in a school within the school. Sustained good standing in this group... must be continually earned by good academic achievement throughout the school year" (December, 2002, p.7). It is easy for students to become part of cliques that separate according to academic achievement. The pressures of fitting in amongst International Baccalaureate students, causes individuals or groups to exclude others and plays a large role in the continuation of cheating and sabotage.

Some schools that have an International Baccalaureate Programme avoid possible segregation by allowing all students to take part in International Baccalaureate classes. "But our school we do not have 'gatekeepers' or policies that exclude students from taking IB or AP courses. This is indeed a shock to some people, because that some IB school students have to 'apply' to take the courses" (Singh, October 2002, p.4). This type of policy can open doors to students who normally would not consider being in the entire International Baccalaureate

Programme that are capable achieving high standards in certain subjects.

When attempting to understand the effects of an International Baccalaureate Programme on the culture of the school, it is important to understand that the information is subjective. Current research supports the fact the International Baccalaureate Programmes intend to promote diversity and acceptance among students and school community. It can be concluded that the International Baccalaureate Programme enhances, challenges, and provides enrichment for its students. Competition and its apparent social and academic effects on the students, however, are still an issue.

The Physical Needs an International Baccalaureate School

In order to provide the elements of diversity, enrichment, and challenge that International Baccalaureate Programmes promote, specific facilities are required. The physical infrastructure of the school covers all the amenities that the school has within its walls. Human resources refer to the expertise provided by staff, faculty, and administration to support the program. In assessing the viability of implementing an International Baccalaureate Programme, schools cannot ignore the significance of rooms, networks, and resources within the school. International Baccalaureate approved schools are expected to provide the following facilities:

-Library media resource centre -Computer lab
-Language rooms - Art room
-Music Room - Theatre/Drama room
-Gallery/Exhibition Place - Gymnasium
- Sports Field - Outdoor Education Facility

These facilities contribute to a dynamic school setting. Multiple types of rooms allow for implementation of a diverse curriculum. While the specific facilities are important considerations, it is possible for a school to manipulate facility use by using one room for many purposes or rotating classes through a facility at different times. The computer lab and the library resource centre, however, are not easily manipulated because of a large role they each play in International Baccalaureate Programmes.

Much of the International Baccalaureate Programme is based on technology. The international world is technologically advanced and teachers and students alike need to use technology for research and work. Within the arena of technology, the International Baccalaureate Programme focuses on several different curriculum areas including: computer science, design technology, and information technology (www.ibo.org). Beyond the technological curriculum, schools must be able to access the online curriculum provided by the International Baccalaureate Organization to reinforce content area instruction. Laptop computers, projectors, and other media play key roles in implementing curriculum. It is essential that schools seeking to host an International Baccalaureate Programme have a state-of-the-art technology center and a technologically literate teaching staff to operate the resources. This resource center must have a sufficient number of computers available to staff and students and provide online networks that support the hardware.

In addition to being computer literate, teachers in an International Baccalaureate Programme must exhibit excellence in teaching, be prepared to commit to International Baccalaureate specific training and professional development, and seek to grow personally and academically. Teachers varied in their expertise are needed to run dynamic classes in the arts, humanities, and sciences. A staff diverse in languages, cultures, and nationalities is essential in developing a strong International Baccalaureate Programme. School districts desiring an International

Baccalaureate Programme not only need to be aware of these requirements, they must be willing and able to commit time and money toward attaining, maintaining, and retaining these resources.

Chapter 4
Research Methods and this Study of International Baccalaureate

This study evaluated current International Baccalaureate Programmes using a mixed methods design that encompassed the acquisition of both qualitative and quantitative data. The purpose of using both forms of data collection was to benefit from the strengths of each type in order to enhance the results of the research (Hittleman & Simon, 2002). Quantitative and qualitative measures are characterized by different techniques for data collection. Aside from the most obvious distinction between numbers and words, the conventional wisdom among evaluators is that qualitative and quantitative methods have different strengths and weaknesses (National Science Foundation, 1997).

Quantitative research is relatively quick to perform and provides precise, numerical data. The data analysis is relatively less time consuming than that of qualitative data and is useful for studying larger groups of people. However, the researcher's categories that are used might not reflect the respondents' understandings. In contrast, qualitative research produces data based on the participants' own categories of meaning and is useful for studying a limited number of cases in depth. Major weaknesses, though, include the facts that the knowledge produced might not generalize to other people or other settings and that the results are more easily influenced by the researchers' personal biases and idiosyncrasies (National Science Foundation, 1997).

Quantitative and qualitative techniques provide a trade-off between breadth and depth, and between the ability to generalize and target specific populations. Mixed methods designs can yield richer, more valid, and more reliable findings than evaluations based on either qualitative or quantitative methods alone. The mixing of methods, or triangulation, allows for diverse standpoints and viewpoints to cast light upon a particular topic. A further advantage is that a mixed methods approach can add insight and understanding that might be missed when only a single method is used. Furthermore, quantitative and qualitative approaches used together can provide stronger evidence for a conclusion through the convergence and corroboration of findings.

Purposeful sampling was used as a selection tool in this study. This is a strategy that serves purposes other than representativeness or randomness. Basic to this type of sampling is the importance of selecting "information-rich" cases from which you can learn much about the issues that are important to the study. The design was to identify teachers and parents of students who were currently involved in International Baccalaureate Programmes. The logic behind this was to partake in an in-depth study of information-rich cases.

School Contexts

Two schools made up the sample for this research: Britannia Secondary Community School and Sir Winston Churchill Secondary School. Britannia and Churchill are both public high schools within the Vancouver School District in Vancouver, British Columbia, Canada.

The Vancouver School District is a large, urban and multicultural school district that includes some of the most affluent and impoverished urban neighbourhoods in Canada. This setting, while providing wonderful opportunities for learning, also provides serious challenges. The district is among the most diverse and complex of all public school systems in Canada, with an annual enrolment of approximately 56,000 students in Kindergarten through Grade Twelve. Of these, 32,000 are elementary school students while the remaining 24,000 are enrolled at the secondary level. District learning sites include 74 elementary schools, 17 elementary annexes, and 18 secondary schools (Vancouver School Board, 2004).

The diversity of the students within the district is remarkable. Fifty-five percent of Kindergarten to Grade twelve students are designated ESL (English as a Second Language) according to Ministry criteria and 61 percent speak a language other than English at home. In fact, 110 different languages have been identified in Vancouver schools. Four percent of elementary and three percent of secondary students are Aboriginal learners. Poverty among children and their families is increasing in the city and the country. The spread of poverty within and outside the borders of what is usually considered Vancouver's inner city has far-reaching consequences for the Vancouver School District. Demands for services to help vulnerable children are continuing to grow. Twelve elementary schools receive district funding as Inner City Schools and sixteen percent of students participate in a school meal programme (Vancouver School Board, 2004).

The programmes and services offered by the Vancouver School District address the combinations of challenge, need, opportunity, and potential that exist in every student. On the one hand, many students living in this urban environment are able to take advantage of opportunities to experience and learn from diverse cultures and reap the benefits of involvement with highly sophisticated and experienced arts and recreational groups. On the other hand, many children, due to poverty and other inhibitors, are excluded from the choices and opportunities that a city the size of Vancouver can offer.

The Schools

Britannia Secondary Community School, which opened in 1908, is the oldest secondary school in Vancouver. It is situated on a 16 hectare site which includes Britannia Elementary School, Hastings Adult Learning Centre, Britannia Community Services Centre, Britannia Community Library (Vancouver Public Library Branch), and a host of recreational, educational, and community services. The over-all administration on site is done cooperatively, by the Britannia Community Services Centre, through a partnership established in 1975 between the Grandview-Woodlands and Strathcona communities, Vancouver City Council, Vancouver School Board, Vancouver Parks Board, and the Vancouver Public Library Board (Vancouver School Board, 2004).

Britannia is a comprehensive community school serving approximately 900 students in grades eight through twelve: 780 students attend class in the main school and about 100 are enrolled in alternative programmes attached to the secondary school. Approximately 190 students are First Nations and 60 students are designated ESL (English as a Second Language) students. The staff is comprised of 56 teachers and 32 support staff members (which includes a community education coordinator, a drug and alcohol counsellor, a school nurse, school support B program workers, a library staff assistant, computer tech support workers, career information assistants, multicultural workers, and First Nations support workers) (Vancouver School Board, 2004).

Britannia is an "inner city school." On a daily basis, there are situations and circumstances often associated with impoverished urban communities. The latest figures show that 31.85 percent of the students live in households that receive income assistance. It is also true that Britannia serves a vibrant community of diverse cultures, interests and needs. Home languages of its students reveal that this diversity is reflected within the student population with at least 38 different languages spoken; English (31%), Chinese (41%), Vietnamese (10%), Spanish (5%), and Tagalog (3%). Britannia's catchment area also has the highest concentration of Aboriginal Peoples in Vancouver (9.5% of the total population) (Vancouver School Board, 2004).

Sir Winston Churchill Secondary School is located in a largely residential neighborhood in south Marpole near Oakridge. It is a comprehensive school of approximately 2,000 students in grades 8 through 12, supported by over 100 teachers. With over 40 first-language groups, the school's student population is decidedly multicultural. Approximately 90% of students choose to attend post-secondary institutions. Consequently, academic excellence is a priority with students and parents and, as a result, many students each year are recognized for their academic achievements. Churchill graduates have received provincial scholarships at a rate in excess of twenty percent of each year's graduating class (Vancouver School Board, 2004).

The feeder schools for Churchill include Sexsmith, David Lloyd George, and Laurier. Sexsmith Community School currently enrolls 410 students reflecting diverse multilingual and multicultural backgrounds. In the school community, there are over twenty different languages spoken. David Lloyd George Elementary School's pupil population represents a wide range of cultural and economic backgrounds. English as a Second Language learners comprise approximately fifty four percent of the student body. There are 28 different languages identified as home languages by the families and there are thirty-one countries listed as the birth countries of its students. Additionally, Lloyd George has a growing number of Eastern European students enrolling. Sir Wilfrid Laurier

Elementary School is located in a community with a combination of upper middle socio-economic level families as well as families in a more transient, socio-economic challenged part of its community. About 75% of the students have a home language other than English. Several families have one parent living and working in Asia. There is strong parent support for school initiatives and good involvement in the Parent Advisory Council (Vancouver School Board, 2004).

In summary, the two schools that were used in the research both demonstrate a strong orientation towards community involvement. Of the two schools, Britannia represents an integrated approach with a site that offers educational services and community programs to all ages. Despite the difference in clientele, Britannia and Churchill are both located in multicultural communities with student populations that speak over 38 and 40 languages, respectively. In terms of socioeconomic status, Churchill is the antithesis of Britannia as it is an affluent residential community with an emphasis on academics and post-secondary transition (see Table 4.1).

Table 4.1
School Summary Table

School Characteristics	**Britannia**	**Churchill**
Emphasis on Community	High	High
Socio-Economic Status	Low	High
Multicultural Population	High	High
Total Student Population	900	2000
Students Pursing Post-Secondary Education	Low	High
Tuition Costs	None	None
Diploma Programme Offered	Yes	Yes
Middle Years Programme Offered	No	Yes

Sample Selection

The two schools that provided the focus for the study were chosen because of the diversity of the clientele that the schools target. Ultimately, Churchill serves a much different clientele than Britannia. Also, another aspect that was taken into consideration was the different components of the International Baccalaureate Programme that the two schools offered (See Table 4.1).

At this point, I feel it is important to mention that I had initially planned on the incorporation of another school in the study, namely Stratford Hall. Stratford Hall is the first school in Western Canada to be authorized by the

International Baccalaureate Organization to teach the Primary Years Programme (PYP). The inclusion of this school would have allowed for a study of all aspects of the International Baccalaureate Programme: the Primary Years Programme, the Middle Years Programme, and the Diploma Programme. Additionally, the addition of Stratford Hall would have allowed this study to illustrate how the International Baccalaureate Programme works in both an independent school (Stratford Hall) and in the public school system (Britannia and Churchill), and the programming issues that may arise based on the different systems. However, Stratford Hall declined to participate in the study.

Britannia offers the International Baccalaureate Programme in grades 11 and 12 only. Prior to this, their own Venture Programme is offered in grades 8 through 10. The Venture programme serves to prepare students for the demands of the International Baccalaureate Programme in grades 11 and 12. Courses include expanded content, as well as the skills necessary to be creative and critical thinkers who can communicate ideas effectively and efficiently. Students interested in the International Baccalaureate Programme are strongly recommended to join the Venture Programme no later than grade 10. Students must make application to both programmes and the school articulates that they are looking for a good academic record, a solid work ethic, and a commitment to activities outside the classroom. Both programmes, says Britannia, offer students unique academic challenges. The school feels that once the students are in university, they will find that the communication and thinking skills they have gained from the International Baccalaureate Programme will help them be successful from the very beginning (Vancouver School Board, 2004).

Churchill offers both the Diploma Programme (grades 11 and 12) and the Middle Years Programme (grades 8 and 9). While the Diploma Programme is a district run programme, the latter is only open to those living within the school's catchment area. Admission to both of these programmes, though, is through application, testing and an interview. For the grade 10 year, students can enroll in the Pre- International Baccalaureate Programme in which they take five grade 10 level International Baccalaureate courses: French, Science, Business Education, Socials and English. Although they are not prerequisites, successful completion of Churchill's Middle Years Programme and Pre-International Baccalaureate Programme are thought to be excellent preparation for the Diploma Programme. Last year, Churchill's International Baccalaureate students achieved the highest results in the history of the program, with a success rate far higher than the world-wide average (Vancouver School Board, 2004).

Interview and Survey Sampling

The initial stage of research involved the surveying of parents and teachers involved in International Baccalaureate Programmes at the afore mentioned schools. During this first part of the study, volunteers were requested to participate in the second, or interview, phase. In order to achieve data that was reflective of the different programmes offered at each school, participants were selected according to the level at which they are involved (see Table 4.2).

Table 4.2

Distributed Survey Breakdown by School, Programme, and Role

School/Programme	Number of Parent Surveys	Number of Teacher Surveys
Britannia/DP	20	10
Churchill/DP	20	10
Churchill/MYP	20	10

The number of parent surveys that were distributed was double the number of teacher surveys. The rationale behind this was that far more parents are involved in International Baccalaureate Programmes than are teachers and this was an important point to highlight. However, so as to appreciate the fact that teachers are directly involved in International Baccalaureate implementation and may, therefore, be more familiar with particular aspects of the programme, this sample group was kept at an unusually high number during this stage of the research.

Survey distribution was accomplished during site visits. In order to target the maximum number of subjects during any given visit, arrangements were made with school principals to attend Parent Advisory Committee meetings, staff meetings, or any other special congregations involving those involved in International Baccalaureate Programmes. Clearly, during the survey distribution phase, the idea of mortality arose. Mortality "refers to a situation where respondents or subjects of a study group drop out for one reason or another" (Glanz, 1998, p.255). In order to increase the response level, my research team and I decided to be present when the surveys were handed out so as to outline the purpose of the research and answer any questions that arose. Also, the IB Coordinators at Britannia and Churchill were extremely helpful in collecting surveys from both parents and teachers. Without this assistance, it is possible that the surveys could have been lost due to a lack of interest from or relevance to the individuals filling in the forms. These actions allowed for the collection of the maximum number of surveys.

During the initial site visits, my research team asked for volunteers to participate in the second phase of research, the interviews. Names and contact numbers were collected so that these individuals could be contacted at a later date to arrange an interview. This stage went into more detail and, therefore, required more time. As a result, the number of subjects involved in the interview phase was fewer than that in the survey phase (see Table 4.3). One or two members of the research team were involved with each interview, depending on the preference of the subject. If two researcher team members were involved, one functioned as the written recorder while the other asked the questions. The rationale behind this was to more accurately record the response. However, if only one researcher was involved, the jobs were combined. All interview responses were typed out as soon as possible after the initial interviews and returned to the respondents so that the transcripts could be checked for accuracy of responses.

Table 4.3

Desired Number of Interviews: Breakdown by School, Programme, and Role

School/ Programme	Number of Parent Interviews	Number of Teacher Interviews
Britannia/DP	2	2
Churchill/DP	2	2
Churchill/MYP	2	2

The reliability of both the quantitative and qualitative research needs to be addressed. A key concept of reliability is whether or not consistent results are seen (Glanz, 1998, p.260). Theoretical reliability refers to the extent that a measure of a concept would deliver the exact same results; no matter how many times it was applied to random members of the same target group. Applied to this study, parallel methods of surveying and interviewing help achieve this goal. It is paramount that surveys be handed out in the same manner. A pre-set and written dialogue or speech for the interviews will assist in keeping these parallels. Another method is to have stratified sampling in which we will look at the subsets such as different socio-economic backgrounds, different age groups, and different sized schools or populations.

Approval for the research occurred in January of 2005. The application to the University of British Columbia Ethics Review Board was submitted and I received approval from the university to proceed with the study. Once clearance was granted, I moved forward and made contact with the Vancouver School District and Stratford Hall. The process then proceeded through the winter months of 2005.

Survey Questions

During the initial stages of my proposal development, I presented a preliminary draft of the survey to fellow Graduate students in the University of British Columbia North Shore Cohort. In light of the feedback generated at that time, insights gained from the literature, and the circumstances of the prospective host districts, I opted to have separate surveys for both teachers and parents. Additionally, questions and responses were altered so as to provide the most useful information in regards to the research questions. I felt that it was important to realize that parents and teachers differ in their knowledge of certain aspects of the programme and designed questions based on this fact. Economic, cultural, academic, and political factors were directly assessed through these questions. The surveys are included in Tables 4.4 and 4.5.

Table 4.4
Parent Survey

International Baccalaureate Parent Survey

Please indicate your type of involvement:
___ DP ___MYP ___PYP

This scale has been prepared so that you can indicate how you feel about the statements below. Please indicate how you feel about each statement.

(SA=Strongly Agree; A=Agree; D=Disagree; SD= Strongly Disagree; DK= Don't Know)

1. The IB Programme meets the academic needs of students. It provides:

	SA	A	D	SD	DK
A challenging curriculum					
Courses that meet local requirements for promotion					
Equal opportunity for all students					
University preparation					

SA A D SD DK   2. The IB Programme adequately prepares my child for standardized tests.

SA   A   D   SD   DK   3. The IB Programme places an emphasis on testing and numerical scores.

SA   A   D   SD   DK   4. IB students have higher than average acceptance rates at post-secondary institutions.

5. The IB Programme better meets the academic needs of students than the following:

	SA	A	D	SD	DK
Advanced Placement (AP)					
Provincial Curriculum					
Other					

SA A D SD DK   6. An IB Programme is an important option for students to have because it allows for diversity in schools.

SA A D SD DK   7. The IB Programme is used to attract new students to the district.

SA A D SD DK   8. The IB Programme serves only a select group of students.

SA A D SD DK   9. The IB Programme excludes the general student population.

SA A D SD DK   10. The additional costs of the IB Programme are justifiable.

The costs are justifiable in the following areas :

	SA	A	D	SD	DK
Admission/Processing Fees					
Yearly tuition fees					
Specialized programming fees					
Material fees					

11. My child's school has sufficient resources to support an IB Programme in the following areas:

	SA	A	D	SD	DK
Computers					
Laptops					
Library resources Periodicals/books					
Internet media					
Qualified Staff					
Fine Art Resources					
Science Lab Resources					

If you had access to more money, where would you put it?

_____

_____

_____

SA A D SD DK   12. My child takes part in regular school activities and is not excluded as a result of his/her involvement in the IB Programme.

13. The general school population has benefited

from the presence of an IB Programme in terms of increased access to:

	SA	A	D	SD	DK
Computer resources/media					
Increased academic programs					
Library resources Periodicals/books					
Better trained staff					
Fine Art Resources					
Science Lab Space / Resources					

If the school could improve in the above areas, what are the top three in terms of priority for change?

1._____
2._____
3._____

SA   A   D   SD   DK   14.   My child was treated equally in the admissions process.

15. To what extent does the IB program affect the school the school's overall academic standards?
A lot ( ) Somewhat ( ) Not at all ( ).

If you feel it affects the school's overall academic standards, please specify how:

_____
_____
_____
_____
_____
_____

16. To what extent does the IB Programme affect the school's entire population?

Academically,

_____
_____
_____

Economically,

_____
_____
_____

Socially,

_____
_____

17. To what extent does the IB Programme address the diverse needs of the students involved?
A lot ( ) Somewhat ( ) Not at all ( ).

Please briefly comment **if** and **how** you feel the following needs are being addressed.
Academic_____
_____
_____

Social_____
_____
_____

Personal/Motivational_____
_____
_____

Thank you for your participation in this survey!

Table 4.5
Teacher Survey

International Baccalaureate Teacher Survey

Please indicate your level of involvement:
___ DP   ___MYP   ___PYP

This scale has been prepared so that you can indicate how you feel about the statements below. Please indicate how you feel about each statement.

(SA=Strongly Agree; A=Agree; D=Disagree; SD= Strongly Disagree; DK= Don't Know)

1. The IB Programme meets the academic needs of students. It provides:

	SA	A	D	SD	DK
A challenging curriculum					
Courses that meet local requirements for promotion					
Equal opportunity for all students					
University preparation					

SA A D SD DK   2. IB students are better prepared than non-IB students for standardized tests.

SA A D SD DK   3. The IB Programme places an emphasis on testing and numerical scores.

SA A D SD DK   4. IB students have higher than average acceptance rates at post-secondary institutions.

SA A D SD DK   5. IB graduates have higher academic success rates than non-IB students at post secondary institutions.

6. The IB Programme better meets the academic needs of students than the following:

	SA	A	D	SD	DK
Advanced Placement (AP)					
Provincial Curriculum					
Other _____ _____					

7. An IB Programme is an important choice for students to have. It provides:

	SA	A	D	SD	DK
Challenging Coursework					
Specialized Courses					
Skill Development					
University Credit					

8. Do you support the following accountability
measures as effective:

	SA	A	D	SD	DK
Teacher workshops					
Evaluation visits					
Other _____ _____					

SA A D SD DK   9. The IB Programme is
used to attract new students to the district.

SA A D SD DK   10. The IB Programme
serves only a select group of students.

SA A D SD DK   11. The IB Programme
excludes the general student population.

SA A D SD DK   12. The school provides
adequate support for the   required IBO professional
development.

Support is provided in the form of:

	SA	A	D	SD	DK
Financial assistance (course fees)					
Financial assistance (travel and accommodat					

	SA	A	D	SD	DK
ion costs)					
Time off					

13. My school has sufficient resources to support an IB Programme in the following areas:

	SA	A	D	SD	DK
Computers					
Laptops					
Library resources Periodicals/books					
Internet media					
Qualified Staff					
Fine Arts Resources					
Science Lab Resources					

If you had access to more money for IB programs, where would you put it?

_____

_____

_____

SA   A   D   SD   DK   14. The entire school population has benefited from the presence of an IB Programme.

SA   A   D   SD   DK   15. The IB Programme has attracted a significant number of out-of-district students to fulfill district enrolment goals.

SA A D SD DK   16. The admissions
process treats all students equally.

17. To what extent does the IB program affect the
school the school's overall academic standards?
    A lot ( ) Somewhat ( ) Not at all ( ).

If you feel it affects the school's overall academic
standards, please specify how:

_____
_____
_____
_____
_____
_____

18. To what extent does the IB Programme affect the
school's entire population?
Academically,_____

_____
_____

Economically,_____

_____
_____

Socially,

_____
_____
_____

19. To what extent does the IB Programme address
the diverse needs of the students involved?
    A lot ( ) Somewhat ( ) Not at all ( ).

Please briefly comment **if** and **how** you feel the
following needs are being addressed.
Academic_____

_____

_____

Social_____

_____

_____

Personal/Motivational_____

_____

_____

Thank you for your participation in this survey!

Interview Questions

     As with the survey questions, the interview questions were also presented to the University of British Columbia North Shore Cohort. Once again, the valuable feedback I received enabled me to increase the clarity of the interview so as to best address the research questions and gain the most pertinent information. Open-ended questions were designed in order to encourage detailed and information-rich responses. Additionally, prior to the beginning of the study, each of my five member research team conducted a pilot interview in order to test the flow and usefulness of the interview questions and to develop their interview techniques. The interview questions are included in Table 4.6.

Table 4.6
Interview Questions
The Interview

1. Please explain your role in relation to the IB Programme.

2. Please explain the length of time you have been involved with and the reasons for your involvement with the IB Programme.

3. Describe the overall costs incurred in the IB Programme.

4. Explain the revenues generated by the school or the district as a result of the IB
   Programme.

5. Describe the typical climate in an IB classroom in your school.

6. Explain the feedback received from the community

(trustees, PAC, other community members) regarding the IB Programme or IB specific activities.

7. Describe how the IB Programme has affected the academic achievement throughout the school.

8. Explain what you feel are the greatest strengths of the IB Programme. Why?

9. Explain what you feel are the greatest weaknesses of the IB Programme. Why?

10. Describe how you would improve the IB Programme in your school.

Analysis

Overall, twenty-four teachers from the two schools provided their views on the IB Programme by participating in the survey part of our research. Each of the respondents was involved in some facet of the IB program (e.g. teaching, administering). The parent surveys were returned by thirty-four of the sixty parents contacted at the two schools. This 57% return rate is above average for a self-administered survey of this type.

In so far as the interview stage of the research was concerned, 2 parents and 8 teachers participated in interviews. These personal interviews covered many of the same themes addressed in the surveys, but were designed to allow for more detailed elaborations on the topics under review.

The employment of both surveys and interviews meant that a plentitude of both quantitative and qualitative data was generated. Although the methods of analysis differed for the two types of data, both provided ways of discerning, examining, comparing and contrasting, and interpreting meaningful patterns or themes.

Assessment is "a process of interpreting information to aid in decision making" (Glanz, 1998, p.246). All five members of my research team performed the assessment aspect of this research study. We worked together and discussed the research that had been generated in order to come to appropriate conclusions. Within this process, I looked at the surveys first and then the interviews. The reasoning behind this was two-fold: first, this was the order in which the data was collected and second, the interviews allowed for the respondents to express themselves in their own words and provided clarity to findings that emerged from the surveys. These aspects helped in my decision-making regarding the conclusions and implications of the study.

Glanz (1998) classifies certain types of research as descriptive and usually characterized by a quantitative approach (p.250). My quantitative research took the form of two surveys that were both comprised of scoring systems that looked at the ways in which people agreed or disagreed (see Table 4.7).

Table 4.7
Survey Responses

Response	Feeling
Strongly Agree (SA)	The participant feels the statement is completely true
Agree (A)	The participant feels that the statement is mostly true
Disagree (D)	The participant feels the statement is not true
Strongly Disagree (SD)	The participant feels the statement is completely untrue
Do Not Know (DK)	The participant is unable to respond due to lack of information

The data collected from these two surveys provided a sufficient information base for the use of statistical analysis techniques. In particular, mean, frequency and percentage scores were used to summarize responses to each of the close-ended questions posed. As well, a consensus index was tabulated to determine the degree of cohesion in the responses offered by the respondents. If 80% of the respondents provided answers in adjacent (e.g. agree and strongly agree, or disagree and strongly disagree) response categories related to a specific question, then strong consensus of opinion on that question was deemed to exist. Lower or general consensus existed if 70% of the responses were in adjacent categories. No consensus was considered apparent if less than a 60% level of cohesion existed. This approach provided a way of interpreting answers that were dispersed among all response categories. Parent and teacher responses were kept separate.

Beyond the close-ended questions, parents and teachers were also provided with opportunities to offer open-ended "top of mind" reactions to each of the IB themes explored. Their comments were recorded verbatim, and then summarized according to recurrent themes. These open-ended comments provided further elaboration on points either highlighted or not addressed directly in the more structured portions of the parent and teacher surveys.

The assessment of the questionnaires was a content analysis that used different categories for classification. Using these factors, I then thoroughly assessed the different factors, namely economic, cultural, academic, and political. However, answers to the research questions not only came from the analysis of the quantitative data. The interviews generated a multitude of qualitative data that we also had to consider.

The interview questions involved the analysis of qualitative data. At a general level, it is necessary to look for patterns and common themes that emerge in responses dealing with specific items. Also, researchers must identify any deviations from these patterns. If deviations exist, factors that might explain these atypical responses can be brought to light. This study adopted the framework developed by Miles and Huberman (1994) to describe the major phases of qualitative data analysis: data reduction, data display, and conclusion drawing.

First, the data had to be organized and somehow meaningfully reduced or reconfigured. Miles and Huberman (1994) describe this stage as data reduction. "Data reduction refers to the process of selecting, focusing, simplifying, abstracting, and transforming the data that appear in written up field notes or transcriptions." Not only does data need to be condensed for the sake of manageability, it also has to be transformed so it can be made intelligible in terms of the issues being addressed. In this study, the notes taken during the interview were written up into what was hoped to be fairly close to verbatim transcripts of the interviews. This took place as soon as possible after the individual interviews so as to provide an accurate transcription of the dialogue.

Data display is the second element in Miles and Huberman's (1994) model of qualitative data analysis. Data display goes a step beyond data reduction to provide "an organized, compressed assembly of information that permits conclusion drawing..." A display can be an extended piece of text or a diagram, chart, or matrix that provides a new way of arranging and thinking about the more textually embedded data. Data displays, whether in word or diagrammatic form, allow the analyst to extrapolate from the data enough to begin to discern systematic patterns and interrelationships. At the display stage, additional, higher order categories or themes may emerge from the data that go beyond those first discovered during the initial process of data reduction. In this study, data matrixes will be employed as often as possible so as to provide clarity and brevity to data display. A sample for the questions, "Explain what you feel are the greatest strengths of the International Baccalaureate Programme?" and "Explain what you feel are the greatest weaknesses of the International Baccalaureate Programme?" has been included in Table 4.8.

Table 4.8
Sample Data Matrix

Respondent Group	Strengths	Weaknesses	Why
Teachers			
Parents			

Conclusion drawing is the third element of qualitative analysis. Conclusion drawing involves stepping back to consider what the analyzed data mean and to assess their implications for the questions at hand. At this point, though, it is important to also consider the quantitative data. Here, I converged and corroborated the findings from both stages of the study. This meant addressing the initial research questions to derive conclusions, implications, and suggestions for future research.

With all of these factors in place, I gained a clear understanding of how effective International Baccalaureate Programmes are in schools. This assessment was intended to ascertain whether North Vancouver would benefit from an International Baccalaureate Programme within its school district.

Chapter 5

A Closer Look at Some Interesting Findings

Introduction

The findings of this research project are based on data collected via three sources of information. The literature review in Chapter 3 provided the theoretical foundation for two systematically structured, self-administered survey questionnaires that were administered to parents and teachers at Britannia Secondary Community School and Sir Winston Churchill Secondary School. Overall, 24 teacher and 34 parent surveys were completed and returned for evaluation. Parent and teacher participants were involved in some aspect of the International Baccalaureate Programme at their school (e.g. teacher, administer, parent). Open-ended questions were recorded verbatim and then summarized according to recurrent themes. Interviews were conducted with 15 participants in an attempt to allow for a more detailed impression of the topics under review.

In the next sections, the findings of my research will be explained through the same lenses that were introduced in our literature review. These are the academic perspective, the economic perspective, the political perspective, the cultural perspective and the physical perspective. Rather than format this chapter solely on research questions, I chose this structure so as to better address those questions that overlap multiple perspectives.

Academic Findings

Do International Baccalaureate Programmes meet the academic needs of North American students and schools? One hundred percent of teachers surveyed in this study agree that the International Baccalaureate Programme provides a challenging curriculum that meets the academic needs of their students. Similarly, 94.1% of parents surveyed agree that the programme provides a challenging curriculum that meets the academic needs of their children. As indicated in Figure 5.1, the majority of both parents and teachers strongly agree and/or agree that the International Baccalaureate Programme offers a challenging program of study in order to meet the academic needs of students.

Figure 5.1. *IB Provides a Challenging Curriculum*

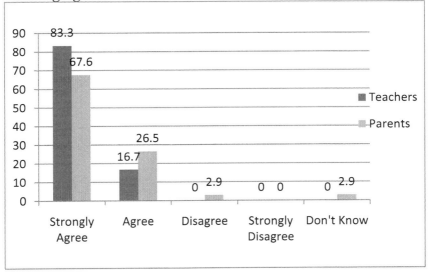

When questioned about local requirements for education, one hundred percent of teachers surveyed agreed that the programme meets the local requirements for promotion. 81.2% of parents surveyed agree. As indicated in Figure 5.2, 79.2% of teachers surveyed strongly agree that the International Baccalaureate Programme meets the local requirement for promotion while 20.8% agree. This result is supported by the parent response rate of 40.6% strongly agree, 40.6% agree, and 18.8% don't know.

Figure 5.2. *IB Meets Local Requirements for Promotion*

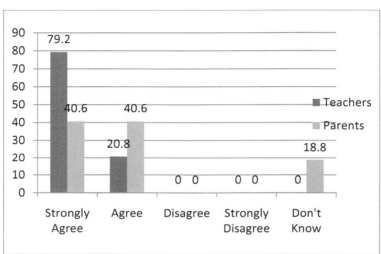

When asked if the programme provides university preparations, again 100% of teachers surveyed agree that the International Baccalaureate Program provides good preparation for university entrance. Parents also responded at a rate of 100%. Figure 5.3 illustrates the response rates of 91.7% of teachers strongly agree while 8.3% agree. The parent response rate was similar with 73.5% strongly agree and 26.5% agree. The responses of teachers and parents surveyed from Britannia Secondary Community School and Sir Winston Churchill Secondary Schools appear to agree with literature presented earlier indicating that the International Baccalaureate Programme does meet the academic needs of schools and students in North America and specifically British Columbia.

Figure 5.3. *IB Provides University Preparation*

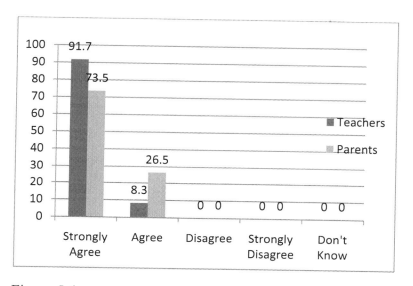

Figure 5.4.
Triangulation of Parent/Teacher Surveys with Research Literature

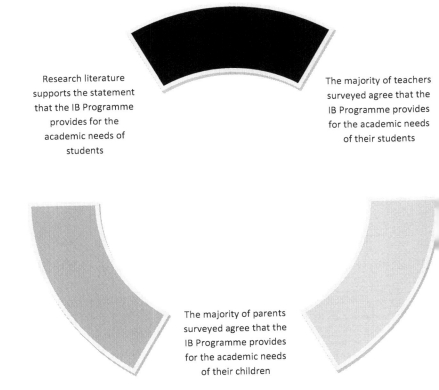

Research literature supports the statement that the IB Programme provides for the academic needs of students

The majority of teachers surveyed agree that the IB Programme provides for the academic needs of their students

The majority of parents surveyed agree that the IB Programme provides for the academic needs of their children

The initial goals of the International Baccalaureate Diploma came from a need to assist international students attain equal footing into world universities and not to realize the educational needs of every student in every part of the world. This original objective initiates questions about elitism, segregation, and the programme's affects on the general student body. The survey asked several questions that address these issues. There are some discrepancies when parents and teachers are asked about student populations served by the International Baccalaureate Programme. Does the International Baccalaureate Programme serve only a select group of students? Figure 5.5 illustrates the differences in beliefs. Of the participants surveyed, 45.8% of teachers and 67.7% of parents agree that the programme serves only a select group of students. These figures are countered with 50% of teachers and 26.5% of parents who disagree with the statement.

The teachers of the survey group were almost evenly split with 8.3% strongly agree, 37.5% agree, 41.7% disagree, 8.3% strongly disagree, and 4.2% don't know. Parents agree with the statement at a higher percentage with 11.8% strongly agree, 55.9% agree, 26.5% disagree, and 5.9% don't know. One teacher at Churchill commented that "it is certainly not a program for everyone."

Figure 5.5. *IB Serves Only a Select Group of Students*

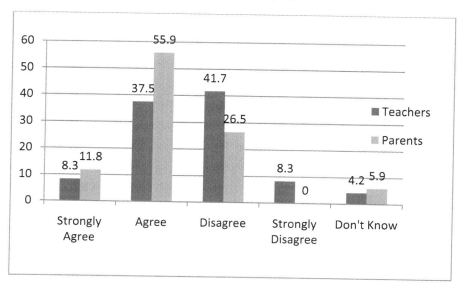

The survey then followed up on this question with the concept of exclusion. When asked if the International Baccalaureate Programme excludes the general student population, there is some disagreement between the participants. Of the teachers surveyed, 70.9% do not believe the programme to be an exclusionary one while only 41.2% of the parents disagree. Teachers and parents rate the programme as exclusionary at a rate of 29.2% (teachers) and 38.2% (parents). Figure 4.6 displays a breakdown of this disagreement. The teacher responses indicated that 12.5% strongly agree, 16.7% agree, 41.7% disagree, and 29.2% strongly disagree with the comment that the International Baccalaureate excludes the general student population. The parent responses to the same statement indicate that 8.8% strongly agree, 29.4% agree, 32.4% disagree, 8.8% strongly disagree, and 20.6% don't know.

Figure 5.6. *IB Excludes the General Student Population*

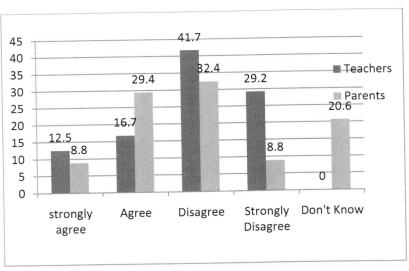

The survey also questioned the academic value of the International Baccalaureate Program to a school by asking the participants to focus on the general population of their school. Has the entire school population benefited from the presence of an International Baccalaureate Program? The majority of the teacher population, 87.5% of the teachers surveyed, indicated that the general population of their school benefits from the presence of the International Baccalaureate Programme. The parent group had the opportunity to specify areas of benefit or lack of benefit. While most indicated a positive statement, it is difficult to get a clear picture of the parent position. Figure 5.7 represents the data provided by the parent group.

Figure 5.7. *Benefit to General Population*

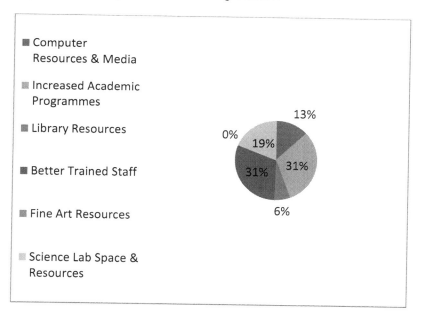

There appears to be a definitive parental perception that the general student population benefits from a better trained staff (31%), increased academic programmes (31%), and additional resources in science labs, computer labs, and the library.

To what extent does the International Baccalaureate Program affect the school's overall academic standards? This question requests teachers and parents to consider the academic benefit of the program at their school to the general population. Interestingly enough, there appears to be some consensus with the perceived benefit to a school with the International Baccalaureate Programme. Both parents and teachers identify positive academic affects for the entire population. Of the teachers surveyed, 65.2% indicated that the programme affects overall achievement "a lot," 26.1% indicated achievement affect as "somewhat," and 8.7% indicated "not at all." Correspondingly, 48.4% of parents indicated "a lot," 45.2% indicated "somewhat" and 6.5% indicated "not at all." Figure 5.8 reveals that the majority of both the teacher and the parent survey groups perceive a benefit of academic achievement as a result of maintaining an International Baccalaureate Programme.

Figure 5.8. *IB Affect on Overall Academic Achievement*

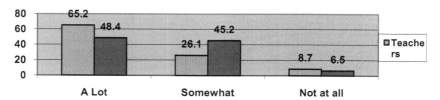

When asked an open ended question about what specific aspects of academic standards and achievements were improved as a result of the International Baccalaureate Program, both teachers and parents praised the high "academic atmosphere" at the school and the high standards and expectations of both teachers and students. This set of outcomes is illustrated in Figure 5.9.

Figure 5.9. *Teacher View/Parent View: Academic Affects*

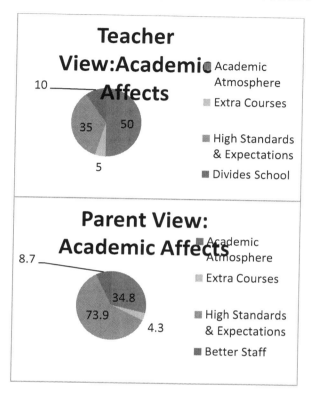

*Multiple responses so percentage may exceed 100%

From an entirely academic viewpoint, the International Baccalaureate Programmes that participated in this study aligned themselves quite well with the literature supporting this topic. Parents and teachers of our survey population believe that the programme offers a challenging curriculum that meets local needs while offering strong preparation for entrance into leading universities. While there are disagreements about issues of academic segregation and exclusion, the International

Baccalaureate Programme is by and large perceived to have a positive affect on the general student population. The programme is perceived to be an academic asset and of great benefit to schools that host them.

Standardized Tests

The issue of standardized tests is a very controversial topic within today's educational field. Although there has been little Canadian research incorporating quantitative data done to compare achievement levels between International Baccalaureate students and students in other programmes, the literature review did reveal some American-based information. International Baccalaureate students outscore the general test-taking population on Scholastic Assessment Tests (SATs) and American College Tests (ACTs) (International Baccalaureate Organization, 2004). However, the literature review revealed no statistical information pertaining to the performance of British Columbian or Canadian International Baccalaureate students compared to the general student population. Accordingly, this section describes parent and teacher perspectives concerning the performance of IB students on standardized tests.

In this study, there was considerable variation in teachers' responses with respect to the statement, "IB students are better prepared than non-IB students for standardized tests" (See Figure 5.10).

Figure 5.10. *IB Students: Are They Prepared for*

Standardized Tests?

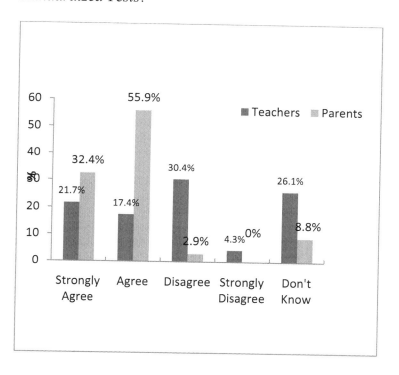

While approximately 39% of teachers agreed that IB students were better prepared, about 35% felt the opposite was the case (See Figure 5.10). It should be noted, however, that 26.1% of teachers did not know the answer to this question. Overall, a lack of consensus seems to exist among the teachers on the matter of student preparation for standardized tests. Responses during the interviews also seemed to be split. While one teacher said, "we are not doing any better with provincial scholarship results because IB students do not write the exams" another said that "the IB students are instrumental in raising the average score on provincial exams."

Parents, however, felt that their children were ready for standardized exams. Over 88% agreed with the notion that "the IB program adequately prepares my child for standardized tests" (See Figure 5.10). A strong consensus on this issue was apparent amongst the parents. This perspective was supported by many open-ended comments. 73.9% of parents felt that there were higher standards when asked how the IB Programme affected the school's overall academic standards. Comments included, "standards are higher for IB students than mainstream - affect ranking amongst other schools" and "the attraction of high achieving students to attend the IB programme definitely brings up the academic achievements of this school."

Clearly, teachers and parents differ in regards to how well they think International Baccalaureate students are prepared for standardized tests. While there is strong consensus amongst parents on this topic, there appears to be much disagreement in the teachers that participated in this study.

Testing and Numerical Scores

The issue of testing and numerical scores is of significant concern for many educational stakeholders. Many feel that it allows outsiders to see "how" the students are doing in particular subject areas. The literature review, though, suggested that the IB Programme prefers to focus on the whole child, and not just individual courses. Many of the characteristics taught in the International Baccalaureate Programme, such as social justice and public responsibility, cannot be easily measured (Singh, 2002; Pajak, 2000). This section describes parent and teacher perspectives concerning the prevalence of testing and numerical scores within the International Baccalaureate Programme.

In this study, teachers disagreed that the International Baccalaureate Programme placed an emphasis on testing and numerical scores (See Figure 5.11).

Figure 5.11. *The IB Programme Places and Emphasis on Testing and Numerical Scores*

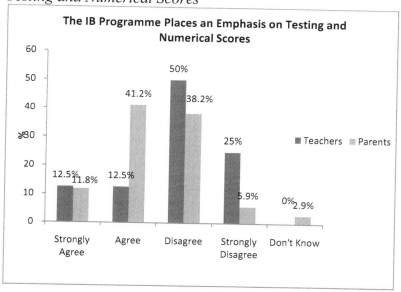

Seventy-five percent or 18 of the teachers disagreed with the notion that the IB Programme highlights marks. A general consensus on this issue was apparent amongst the teachers. This perspective was supported by many of their interview comments. When asked what they thought were the greatest strengths of the IB Programme, teacher comments included, "The programme's focus on the whole child" and "the programme is not just academic, it focuses on producing well-rounded people."

The parents, however, were undecided as to whether or not the IB Programme placed an emphasis on testing and numerical scores (See Figure 5.11). Although the slim majority felt that this was indeed the case (53%), 44% felt that this was untrue. Overall, no consensus existed amongst the parents' survey responses in regards to this matter. In contrast, though, the parent's open-ended responses seemed to emphasize the IB Programme's focus on the whole person. One parent said, "They work on the student as a whole person. My son has increased his level of confidence as a result of being in the programme" while another said that, "IB is not mark centered. IB emphasizes to help students to develop as a whole person." However, one parent did bring up what they perceived to be the programme's focus on marks: "Students are required to have good grades in order to enter into IB, and then the students are required to keep grades up."

Clearly, teachers and parents cannot come to a general consensus on whether or not they think that the International Baccalaureate Programme places an emphasis on testing and numerical scores. Although teachers disagreed with this statement, parents were split on this point.

Post-Secondary Acceptance Rates

University acceptance rates are of significant concern to many educational stakeholders. In its own study, the International Baccalaureate Organization compared the acceptance rates for International Baccalaureate students as compared to the overall acceptance rate published by individual colleges and universities. International Baccalaureate students were accepted at a much higher rate than the total population (IBO, 2004). Additionally, Matthews (2003) claimed that, "IB [has] acquired the status of [a] backstage pass at a rock concert." Without a doubt, the literature review strongly suggested that IB students are accepted at a much higher rate into post-secondary institutions than are non-IB students. The following section describes parent and teacher perspectives concerning the acceptance rates of International Baccalaureate students at post-secondary institutions.

In this study, the teachers overwhelmingly agreed that International Baccalaureate students have higher than average acceptance rates at post-secondary institutions (See Figure 5.12).

Figure 5.12. *IB Students Have Higher Than Average Acceptance Rates at University*

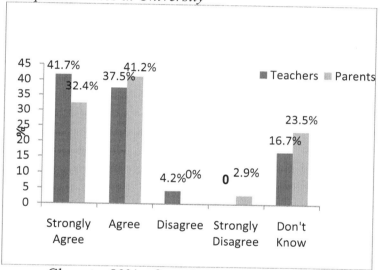

Close to 80% of teachers agreed with this notion, while only 4% disagreed. Also interesting, though, is the fact that almost 17% of teachers did not know the answer to this question. However, a high level of general consensus on this issue was apparent among teachers.

Like the teachers, the parents also agreed that IB students have higher than average acceptance rates at post-secondary institutions (See Figure 5.11). Of the parents surveyed, 74% agreed with this notion, while only 2.9% disagreed. Again, there was an extremely high percentage of respondents that did not know the answer to this question. Among the parents, this was almost 24%. However, there was still a general consensus on this issue among parents.

In short, this study indicated that while the majority of parents and teachers believe International Baccalaureate students are getting into universities at rates higher than non- International Baccalaureate students, a large number of parents and teachers do not know if this is the case.

IB Graduates Have Higher Academic Success Rates than Non-IB Students at Post-Secondary Institutions

Life-long learning is an issue that is prominent in today's educational discussions. The literature review suggested that International Baccalaureate graduates continue to perform well into their university years. The United States Department of Education recognized that participation in a rigorous curriculum like that of IB predicts whether a student will graduate from college (U.S. Department of Education, 1999). Other authors stated that International Baccalaureate students outperform non-International Baccalaureate students in college and university (Daniel & Cox, 1992; Thomas, 1998). The following section describes parent and teacher perspectives concerning the performance of IB students once they are registered in post-secondary institutions.

Did the twenty-four teachers who participated in the survey agree when questioned about the post secondary success rate of International Baccalaureate students? Yes, they did. The teachers agreed that IB graduates have higher academic success rates than non-IB students at post secondary institutions (See Figure 5.13).

Figure 5.13. *IB Graduates Success Rates at Post Secondary Institutions*

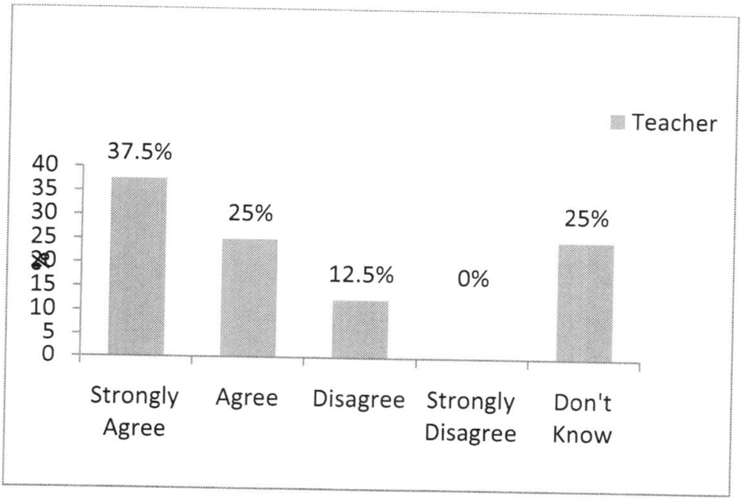

Although 62.5% agreed with the notion, there were still 12.5% who did not. Additionally, 25% of respondents claimed that they did not know. Due to the low level of cohesion, the survey results do not clearly indicate teachers' perceptions on this topic. Open-ended results, though, seemed to favor International Baccalaureate graduates once they reached university. Comments included "Students learn to write formal essays and by the time they get to university, they are way ahead of other first year students".

Comparison of the IB Programme with Other Programmes

With so much competition existing in education today, it is only natural that there is competition amongst the various programmes that are offered in schools. Although there is some qualitative literature that compares the International Baccalaureate

Programme with the Advanced Placement Programme in regards to their overall aims (Freeman, 1987; IBO and College Board, 2002), there is little quantitative data of this nature. This next section describes parent and teacher perspectives concerning the comparison of International Baccalaureate with Advanced Placement and the provincial curriculum.

Teachers agreed that the International Baccalaureate Programme better meets the academic needs of students than does Advanced Placement (See Figure 5.14). Of the teachers surveyed, 58.3% agreed with this statement while only 4.2% disagreed. Interesting, though, is the percentage of respondents who indicated that they did not know (37.5%). Although more than half of the teachers agreed with this statement, no statistical consensus was apparent among the teachers. Teachers' open-ended responses failed to mention the Advanced Placement Programme.

Figure 5.14. *IB Better Meets the Needs of Students Than Does AP*

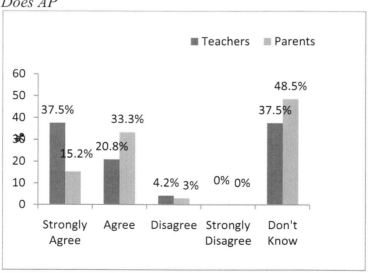

Parents also agreed that the International Baccalaureate Programme better meets the academic needs of students than does Advanced Placement (See Figure 5.14). In this case, almost half agreed with this statement while only 3% disagreed. Again, though, there is an extremely high percentage of respondents who indicated that they did not know (48.5%). Based on these percentages, consensus cannot be said to exist. Once again, there was no mention of Advanced Placement courses during open-ended responses by parents.

In regards to the question of whether the International Baccalaureate Programme better meets the academic needs of students than does the provincial curriculum, the teachers once again agreed with this statement (See Figure 5.15).

Figure 5.15. *IB Better Meets the Needs of Students Than Does the Provincial Exams*

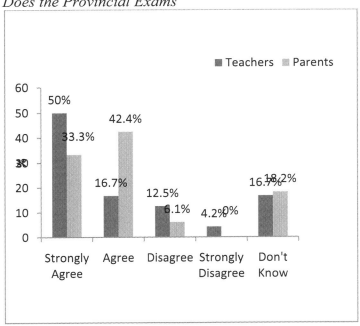

Almost sixty-seven percent agreed, while 16.7% disagreed. This percentage happens to match with the percentage of respondents who indicated that they did not know (16.7%). Teacher comments that compared the IB Programme to the regular academic offering were positive and included, "Students who may be bored with the limited demands of the provincial curriculum are challenged," "IB students are challenged academically to a much greater extent than they would be in a regular classroom," "Historically, students not successful in regular programs have excelled here," and "A lot of these kids may not perform nearly as well in regular classes."

The parents felt that the International Baccalaureate Programme better meets the academic needs of students than does the provincial curriculum (See Figure 5.15). Seventy-six percent agreed with this statement while only 6.1% disagreed. A general consensus can be said to exist amongst parents in regards to this issue. The comments made by parents were also positive and included, "IB students are more challenged in their studies…"

So, although there are a large number of parents and teachers who do not know if the International Baccalaureate Programme better meets the needs of students than does Advanced Placement or the provincial curriculum, the majority of those questioned do, in fact, feel that this is the case.

Academic Results Summary

In looking at the academic results as a whole, teachers and parents are generally positive about the International Baccalaureate Programme. They feel that not only does the International Baccalaureate Programme meet the local requirements for promotion, but the International Baccalaureate curriculum exceeds the provincial curriculum and other academic options such as Advanced Placement. Additionally, the International Baccalaureate Programme prepares students for university, grants them post-secondary acceptance at rates higher than the general population, and allows for continued success once they are attending university. Clearly, parents and teachers both expressed positive sentiments in their assessment of the International Baccalaureate Programme's academic merits.

Findings on the Economic Perspective

Choice

Open enrolment is an important topic for many school districts as it can potentially be linked to a school's economic survival. With parents being given the ability to choose a school, despite neighborhood boundaries, the International Baccalaureate programme provides the financial and academic means to attract and keep new and current students.

In this study, teachers overwhelmingly agreed that an International Baccalaureate programme is an important choice for students to have. The question was further broken down by challenging coursework (mean = 3.79), specialized courses (mean = 3.65), skill development (mean = 3.70), and university credit (mean = 3.59). Clearly, a general consensus on this issue was evident among the teachers with a very low percentage of respondents that did not know the answer to this question. The teachers' open ended responses mainly focused on the programme's ability to offer more than the traditional curriculum. Some of the teachers' comments included "higher level and standard level choices that allow students to focus on their strengths." Another teacher noted "the wide range of activities required and the diverse types of assessments and evaluations encourage many talents and call on many learning and teaching styles." Teacher perceptions of the importance of the choice of the International Baccalaureate Programme are reported in Table 5.1.

Table 5.1
Teacher: An IB Programme is an important choice for students to have.

IB Programmes provide:

a. Challenging Coursework

Response	n	%
Strongly agree	19	79.2
Agree	5	20.8
Disagree	0	0.0
Strongly disagree	0	0.0
Don't know	0	0.0
N	24	100.0

b. Specialized Courses

Response	n	%
Strongly agree	16	66.7
Agree	6	25.0

Disagree	1	4.2
Strongly disagree	0	0.0
Don't know	1	4.2
N	24	100.0

c. Skill Development

Response	n	%
Strongly agree	17	70.8
Agree	5	20.8
Disagree	1	4.2
Strongly disagree	0	0.0
Don't know	1	4.2
N	24	100.0

d. University Credit

Response	n	%
Strongly agree	16	66.7
Agree	3	12.5
Disagree	3	12.5
Strongly disagree	0	0.0

Don't know	2	8.3
N	24	100.0

Summary:

Category	Mean*	n
Challenging Coursework	3.79	24
Specialized Courses	3.65	23
Skill Development	3.70	23
University Credit	3.59	22

* Based on a scale where 1 = strongly disagree, 2 = disagree, 3 = agree and 4 = strongly agree. "Don't know" responses excluded from calculation of mean. The higher the mean, the greater is the level of agreement.

Figure 5.16 illustrates that teachers reached consensus on the ability of the International Baccalaureate Programme to offer challenging coursework, specialized courses, a focus on skill development, and an opportunity for university credit. In terms of the ability for an International Baccalaureate Programme to attract new students to the district, the responses of the study were mixed and inconclusive. It is important to note that 70.6% of parents felt that the IB programme is used to attract new students to the district while only 58.3% of teachers felt the same way (Table 5.2, Table 5.3, and Figure 5.17).

Figure 5.16. *The International Baccalaureate and Choice*

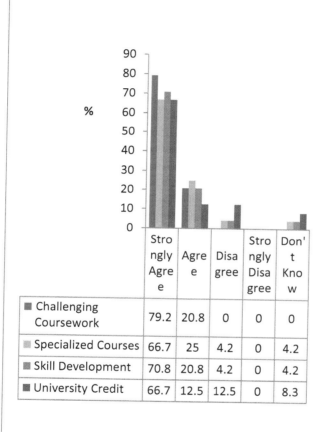

	Strongly Agree	Agree	Disagree	Strongly Disagree	Don't Know
Challenging Coursework	79.2	20.8	0	0	0
Specialized Courses	66.7	25	4.2	0	4.2
Skill Development	70.8	20.8	4.2	0	4.2
University Credit	66.7	12.5	12.5	0	8.3

Table 5.2

Parent: The IB Programme is used to attract new students to the district.

Response	n	%
Strongly agree	5	14.7
Agree	19	55.9
Disagree	7	20.6
Strongly disagree	0	0.0
Don't know	3	8.8
N	34	100.0
Average*	2.94	31

Table 5.3

Teacher: The IB Programme is used to attract new students to the district

Response	n	%
Strongly agree	5	20.8
Agree	9	37.5
Disagree	6	25.0
Strongly disagree	1	4.2
Don't know	3	12.5
N	24	100.0
Average*	2.86	N=21

- Based on a scale where 1 = strongly disagree, 2 = disagree, 3 = agree and 4 = strongly agree. "Don't know" responses excluded from calculation of mean. The higher the mean, the greater is the level of agreement.

Figure 5.17. *The Ability IB to Attract New Students*

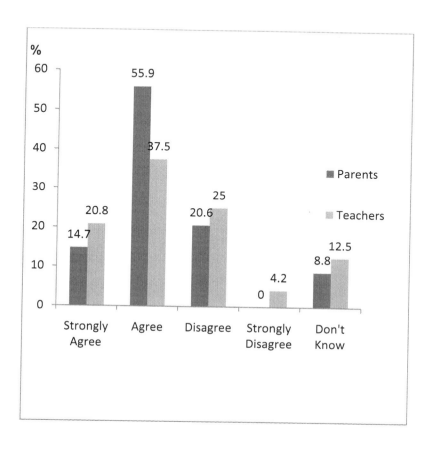

This data proved inconclusive in determining the ability of the International Baccalaureate Programme to attract out-of-district students. Additionally, the study rephrased the question for teachers and the responses were still inconclusive. Only 33.4% of teachers agreed that the International Baccalaureate Programme has attracted a significant number of out-of-district students. It is important to note that 33.3% of teachers did not know the answer to this question (Table 5.4).

Table 5.4

Teachers: The IB Programme has attracted a significant number of out-of-district students to fulfill district enrolment goals

Response	n	%
Strongly agree	1	4.2
Agree	7	29.2
Disagree	6	25.0
Strongly disagree	2	8.3
Don't know	8	33.3
N	24	100.0
Average	2.44	N=16

Cost Analysis

With the tremendous costs attached to implementing and sustaining an International Baccalaureate Programme, school districts must consider if these costs are justifiable. Central to this discussion is how parents will feel with any costs that they will have to incur. In this study, parents (mean = 2.96) did not reach consensus when asked if the additional costs of the International Baccalaureate Programme are deserved. Again, a high percentage of parents (20.7%) did not feel they could answer this question (Table 5.5).

Table 5.5
Parents: The additional costs of the IB Programme are justifiable.

Response	n	%
Strongly agree	6	20.7
Agree	12	41.4
Disagree	3	10.3
Strongly disagree	2	6.9
Don't know	6	20.7
n	29	100.0
Average	2.96	23

The study further broke down the same question into the following fees: admission/processing; yearly tuition; specialized programming, and material fees. Three out of the four categories yielded an inconclusive mean to make any decisive observations. Specialized programming fees (mean = 3.00) was the only criterion that parents (64.5%) felt were justifiable additional costs. Again, an alarming 25.8% could not answer this question (Table 5.6).

Table 5.6
Justifiable International Baccalaureate Cost
The costs are justifiable in the following areas:
a. Admission/Processing Fees

Response	n	%
Strongly agree	5	16.1
Agree	13	41.9
Disagree	5	16.1
Strongly disagree	3	9.7
Don't know	5	16.1
n	31	100.0

b. Yearly tuition fees

Response	n	%
Strongly agree	5	16.1
Agree	11	35.5
Disagree	5	16.1
Strongly disagree	3	9.7
Don't know	7	22.6
n	31	100.0

c. Specialized programming fees

Response	n	%
Strongly agree	5	16.1
Agree	15	48.4
Disagree	1	3.2
Strongly disagree	2	6.5
Don't know	8	25.8
n	31	100.0

d. Material fees

Response	n	%
Strongly agree	4	12.5
Agree	17	53.1
Disagree	1	3.1
Strongly disagree	3	9.4
Don't know	7	21.9
n	32	100.0

e. Summary of fee responses

Area	Mean*	n
Admission/Processing Fees	2.77	26
Yearly tuition fees	2.75	24
Specialized programming fees	3.00	23
Material fees	2.88	25

During the interviews, participants were asked: To what extent does the International Baccalaureate programme economically affect the entire school population? Both the parent and teacher responses demonstrated an uncertain tone to the economic perspective. Some of the teacher responses ranged from, "it probably taxes it (school population) – professional development, field trips, etc. but I'm not sure" to "this is like an expensive private education, only better in every aspect." The parent responses, which included 23% of 'don't know' responses, ranged from "more funding is given" to "not at all." Undoubtedly, this is an area for further research. Figure 5.18 illustrates participant positions on the justifiability of the fees incurred by the International Baccalaureate Programme.

Figure 5.18. *Are IB Fees Justifiable or Not?*

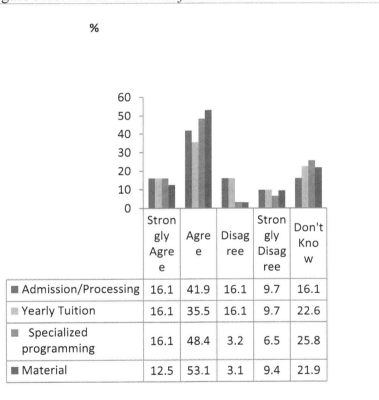

	Strongly Agree	Agree	Disagree	Strongly Disagree	Don't Know
▓ Admission/Processing	16.1	41.9	16.1	9.7	16.1
▓ Yearly Tuition	16.1	35.5	16.1	9.7	22.6
▓ Specialized programming	16.1	48.4	3.2	6.5	25.8
▓ Material	12.5	53.1	3.1	9.4	21.9

Accountability

In Chapter III, the literature review demonstrated an emergence of a client (market) and contractual accountability (Poulson, 1998) that was externally imposed on education with the assumption that the use of business strategies would be the best method to reform education equating to an emphasis on quantitative measures. The literature review suggested that despite the external accountability measures and a certain degree of standardization, stakeholders were generally supportive. In this study, teachers supported the client accountability practices and characterized them as effective. The two accountability measures, teacher workshops (mean = 3.35) and evaluation visits (mean = 3.00), were seen as useful in their schools. Approximately 91.7% agreed that teacher workshops were effective, while approximately 61% agreed that evaluation visits were useful. Conversely, only 4.2% disagreed that teacher workshops were ineffective and an 8.6% disagreement rate for evaluation visits. It should be noted, however, that 4.2% did not know the answer for the effectiveness of teacher workshops and 30.4% were unable to explain the effectiveness of evaluation visits for their schools (Table 5.7 and Figure 5.19).

Table 5.7
Teacher Support for Accountability Measures
Teacher: Do you support the following accountability measures as effective:
a. Teacher workshops

Response	n	%
Strongly agree	9	37.5
Agree	13	54.2
Disagree	1	4.2
Strongly disagree	0	0.0
Don't know	1	4.2
n	24	100.0

b. Evaluation visits

Response	n	%
Strongly agree	3	13.0
Agree	11	47.8
Disagree	1	4.3
Strongly disagree	1	4.3
Don't know	7	30.4
n	23	100.0

Summary:

Measures	Mean*	N
Teacher workshops	3.35	23
Evaluation visits	3.00	16

Based on a scale where 1 = strongly disagree, 2 = disagree, 3 = agree and 4 = strongly agree. "Don't know" responses excluded from calculation of mean. The higher the mean, the greater is the level of agreement.

Figure 5.19. *Affective Measure of Accountability*

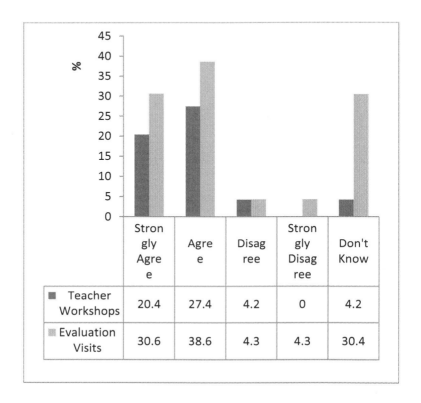

	Strongly Agree	Agree	Disagree	Strongly Disagree	Don't Know
■ Teacher Workshops	20.4	27.4	4.2	0	4.2
■ Evaluation Visits	30.6	38.6	4.3	4.3	30.4

In terms of contractual accountability, the study looked at the reported emphasis on testing and numerical scores (quantitative indicators). As stated in the finding of the academic section, teachers generally disagreed that the International Baccalaureate Programme places an emphasis on testing and numerical scores. The parents, however, were unresolved in this matter. Nevertheless, it was clear from a teachers' perspective that an emphasis on quantitative measures, like testing and numerical scores, did not exist which was contrary to the literature review. It should be noted that the literature review also found that a school's professional accountability and flexibility could counter any hegemonic sentiments.

The Effect of the IB Programme on the School Culture

This section describes parent and teacher perspectives concerning the perceived effects of International Baccalaureate programmes on overall school culture. In particular, it explores the themes of segregation, diversity and competitiveness that were identified as potential impacts in the literature. In order to ensure an accurate depiction of current perspectives on each of these themes, the views of both teachers and parents are independently summarized and then compared with findings in the literature.

The Possibility of Segregation

The issue of segregation versus integration of International Baccalaureate students within overall school culture is a significant concern for many education stakeholders. The literature review suggested that students within International Baccalaureate Programmes consider themselves to be attending a school within a school.

In this study, on average the parents surveyed were undecided with respect to whether or not International Baccalaureate Programmes tended to create segregation between their children and other pupils at the schools (e.g, mean score = 2.48). Parents were asked if the program excludes the general student population and about 30% of the parents agreed that segregation of International Baccalaureate students occurred, while another 32% of them felt that this was not the case. Overall, no consensus existed among the parents on this matter. In contrast, open-ended responses were generally positive with respect to the segregation effects of International Baccalaureate

Programmes. A full 80% of the open ended comments expressed positive views on International Baccalaureate Programme affects. For instance, one parent suggested that "IB students are responsible for the running of many clubs and events", while another indicated that the IB program had created "a small tight knit group, who generally stay out of trouble and contribute to school clubs" (Figure 5.20). Figure 5.20. *How does the IB Programme Affect the School Population? - Parents*

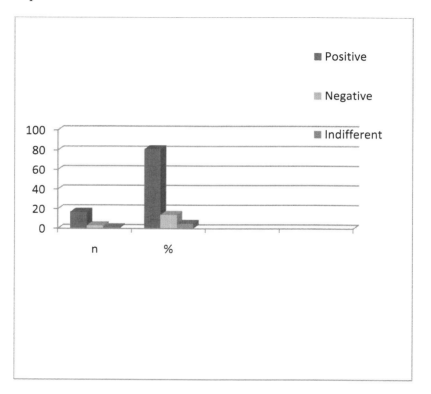

On average, teachers disagreed that the International Baccalaureate Programmes created a segregated environment for students (mean=2.13). Almost 70% disagreed with the notion that the International Baccalaureate Programme created this exclusion among students. A general consensus on this issue was apparent among the teachers (Table 5.21). Indeed, 45% of the open-ended comments received from teachers suggested that the International Baccalaureate Programme promoted student leadership within the entire school. Another 10% of the comments indicated that the programme created greater diversity in the school's population and activities. However, there were conflicting voices among teachers concerning whether segregation created by International Baccalaureate programs was a positive or negative connotation (Figure 5.21).

Figure 5.21. *How Does the IB Programme Affect the School Population? - Teacher*

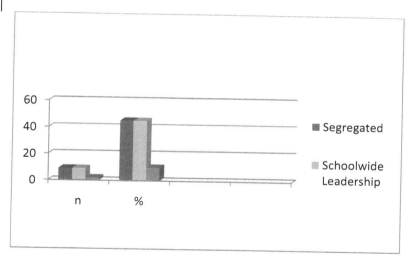

Diversity

The literature review sources discussed that a goal of the IB programme was to promote diversity among its participants. It suggested that the program provided many different avenues for the students to gain an education that encompassed aspects such as group work, leadership opportunities, and community involvement. On average, when asked if the student's diverse needs were being met, parents agreed. Using the scale of a lot, somewhat, or not at all, half the parents said 'a lot' while the other half said 'somewhat'. None of the parents filled in the not at all category. When discussing how the student's social needs were being met in IB, 53% of the parent's open ended responses stated cohesion and social events, 40% said

environmental and community issues. The remaining comments centered on the student's exposure to social issues (Table 5.8). Comments that typify the type of cohesion among the group were ones related to the group work. One respondent said, "The students are a tight knit group. Group projects and retreats contribute to healthy social interactions."

Table 5.8 *How Do Students Gain Diversity? - Parents*

Category	Parent nf	Percentage
Cohesion/ Social Events	8	53.3
Exposure to Social Issues	2	13.3
Environmental/Community Issues	6	40
Encourages Responsibility	1	6.7
Total	17	113.3

When teachers were surveyed on the extent to which the students diverse needs were being met, they responded overwhelmingly in the "a lot" category (73%) with 22% claiming only "somewhat" (Table 5.9). The teachers believe that socially these students gain this diversity through student support (58%), community global awareness (11%), and school program support (42.1%) (Table 5.9). The open-ended responses focused on the IB groupings in particular, with comments such as, "They are a tight knit group who support each other," and "Students are widely accepted within the group". There is a strong consensus amongst both the parents and the teachers with regards to diversity. There is a triangulation here because there is agreement by both teachers and parents through comments and through the survey instruments. The majority of the participants agreed with current literature that International Baccalaureate students gain diversity through student support, the program, and a focus on global issues.

Table 5.9

How Do Students Gain Diversity? – Teachers

Category	Teacher nf	Percentage
Student Support	11	57.9
Global Awareness	2	10.5
School Program Support	8	42.1
Total	21	110.5

Competitiveness among Students

Cheating, overwhelming amounts of work, and an advanced and difficult curriculum were highlighted in the literature review. This study analyzed the effects of competitiveness using open–ended questions about the personal and motivational aspects of International Baccalaureate programmes. The responses were broken down into three categories: peer support, personal motivation, and leadership opportunities. There were multiple responses available so some of the percentages were able to exceed 100% of the respondent totals. The most dominant response for both parents (47%) and teachers (56%) was that the programme promoted the group mentality of the students in the International Baccalaureate Programme. The parents had responses such as, "Group pressure makes the students more motivated and challenged," and "Students feel motivated by being part of the IB community." The teachers re-enforced this idea with statements like, "Students motivate each other and recognize similar stresses and create a support network." The notion of group support was a key theme in the responses.

Personal motivation was another dominant issue. It is apparent that students need to be self-motivated and independent learners as over 40% of respondents in the teacher and parent categories stated that the large workload needs to be managed effectively. Parents responded with "Students develop an excellent work ethic," and students "learn to cope with the workload." Teachers confirm the issue of workload with statements such as, "Students are driven to personal excellence" and they "encourage each other to keep up with the workload."

Parents, in particular, focused on the importance of leadership opportunities for International Baccalaureate students. While the literature did not identify this as an important factor, 40% of parents surveyed in this study were interested in the significance of leadership opportunities. Only 6% of teachers made reference to this issue. The parents mentioned the CAS (Creativity/Action/Service) requirement and the need to get involved in the community and school.

A Summary on the Cultural Perspective

The cultural characteristics of a school are included in many of the reflective features of this study. Not only does the study examine how students and teachers are affected in the school, it looks at the broader picture of how the attitudes within a school are affected. The cultural aspect is woven into the political and academic aspects of the study. Many of the attitudes and issues that concern academic and political realms rely on student motivation. The feelings within a school, personal and group motivation, peer support, leadership opportunities, attitudes, stress, and identity perceptions are important considerations. These are clearly important issues for parents and teachers involved with these International Baccalaureate Programmes.

Political Implications and Effects of the International Baccalaureate Programme

This section addresses some of the political implications and effects of the International Baccalaureate Programme. In particular, it explores the issues of opportunity; diversity; admissions requirements; and sustainability.

Opportunity for Students

According to the literature, there are many contentious issues surrounding the topic of school choice (Brayne, 2004: Ryan and Heise, 2002; Richmond School District, 2001; Hill, 1996; Viteretti, 1996). The term itself is fraught with multiple meanings and interpretations. The majority of the literature tends to define choice as falling into four basic clusters along a continuum –ranging from personal control at one end to voucher programmes at the other. While this is a simplistic way to define choice programmes, it is also problematic. Many 'choice' programmes do not fall neatly into one of the four clusters, and may actually overlap. Such is the case with the International Baccalaureate Programme. It is often thought of as an alternate programme, though it also falls under the cluster of open boundaries. This information is important to keep in mind when interpreting the results of the data surrounding opportunity for students.

The survey results indicate that 84.9% of parents felt that the International Baccalaureate Programme is an important option for students to have (Figure 5.22). Likewise, the majority of teachers felt the International Baccalaureate Programme is an important choice as it provides challenging coursework (100%); Specialized Courses (91.7%), Skill Development (91.6%), and University Credit (79.2%). The results clearly indicate that both parents and teachers feel strongly that the International Baccalaureate Programme is an important choice for students to have, an important programme to offer to students, and feel that the programme meets the needs of many students.

Figure 5.22. *An IB Programme is an Important Option for Students to Have*

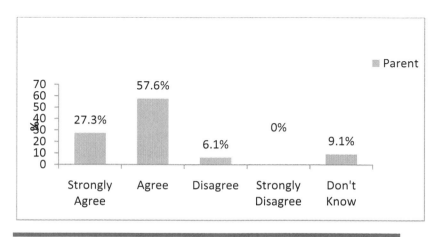

Diversity

The literature review addressed the claim that the International Baccalaureate Programme is elitist (Ryan and Heise, 2002; Hill, 1996; Herron, 1985). The majority of the literature indicated that this claim may have been valid when the International Baccalaureate Programme was first implemented in 1968, however the literature now points to the fact that the International Baccalaureate Organization is committed to making an International Baccalaureate Education available to students from all types of backgrounds, and that 90 per cent of schools offering the International Baccalaureate Programme are public schools that serve all types of students (http://www.ibo.org).

Results from the parent surveys (Figure 5.23) indicated that 91.2% of parents feel that the International Baccalaureate Programme offers equal opportunity for all students. Interestingly, when asked if the International Baccalaureate Programme serves only a select group of students 67.7% of parents felt it did, while 26.5% stated that it did not. Additionally, 38.2% felt that the International Baccalaureate Programme excludes the general population, while 41.2% felt that it did not.

Figure 5.23. *Who Does the IB Programme Serve? - Parents*

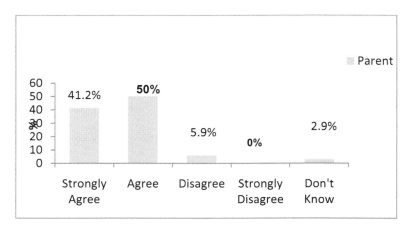

When looking at the same questions for teachers, the results show that seventy-five percent of teachers indicated that the International Baccalaureate Programme provides equal opportunity for all students. However, when asked if the International Baccalaureate Programme serves only a select group of students, the results were mixed (45.8% felt it did; while 50% felt it did not). When asked if the International Baccalaureate Programme excludes the general student population, 29.2% felt it did, while the majority (70.8%) felt that it did not. Figure 5.24 details the results from teacher survey.

Figure 5.24. *Who Does the IB Program Serve? - Teachers*

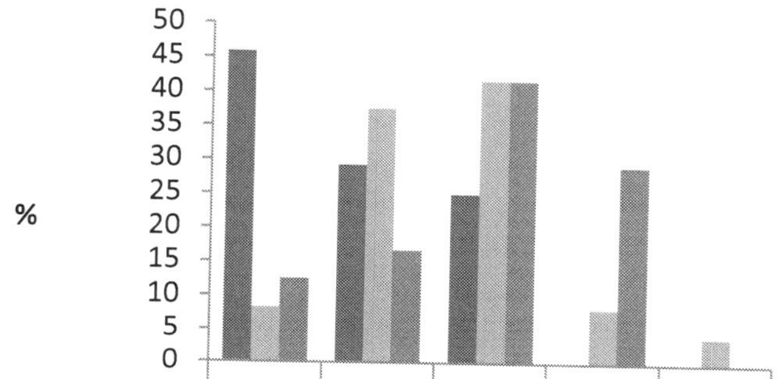

	Strongly Agree	Agree	Disagree	Strongly Disagree	Don't Know
▪ Equal Opportunity	45.8	29.2	25	0	0
▫ Select Group	8.3	37.5	41.7	8.3	4.2
▪ Excludes the general population	12.5	16.7	41.7	29.2	0

Admissions Requirements

As evidenced in the literature, each school offering an International Baccalaureate Programme is responsible for establishing its own admission requirements. As such, there are tremendous variations in admission requirements. In this study, it appears that the majority of parents surveyed (90.3%) felt that their child was treated equally in the admissions process. As well, the majority of teachers surveyed felt strongly that all students were treated equally (91.6%). This is illustrated in Figure 5.25.

Figure 5.25. *Admissions Process Treats All Student Equally*

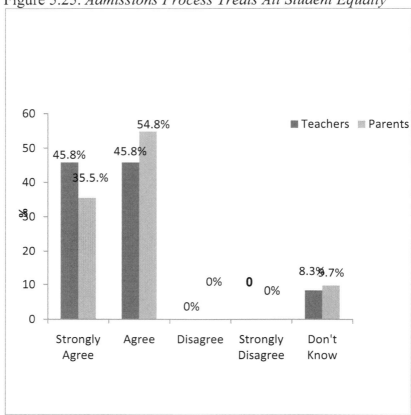

The data collected in this study indicate that an overwhelming majority of parents and teachers feel that the admissions process is fair and equitable. Due to the fact that the admissions process varies between schools, the results are site specific, and if asked the same question concerning the admissions process at a different school, the results may have been quite different. However, in this particular study, the consensus among parents and teachers was that the admissions process treats all students equally. The interview responses strongly suggest that students accepted into the programme deserve to be there, are high calibre students, and are not there on the basis of marks alone. The following response illustrates the tone of the comments "...students who get accepted into the IB programme are enthusiastic, high achieving students within the school as a whole, who can encourage and motivate all."

Sustainability of the International Baccalaureate
Programme

The literature indicates that in order for an International Baccalaureate Programme to be successful, it will need to attract a given number of students (Hill, 1996). In this study, 70.6% of parents felt that the International Baccalaureate Programme was a determining factor in attracting new students to the district. Teachers, however, felt less strongly about the force of the International Baccalaureate Programme to attract new students. Only 58.3% of teachers felt the programme was used to attract new students (Figure 5.26). The results are interesting in light of the fact that in Vancouver, the cost of the International Baccalaureate Programme is subsidized by the Vancouver School Board, so the programme is not a revenue generating tool in Vancouver. The fact that the programme is operating at two distinctly different schools within the Vancouver School Board, does however, attract students to those particular schools who are interested in the programme. Many of the students currently involved in the International Baccalaureate Programme at Churchill and Britannia come from out of catchment area/out-of-district, solely to partake in the programme. The success and popularity of the programme has increased dramatically since the initial implementation more than twenty years ago at Churchill Secondary. The interview data provides information about the success of the programme. It indicates that the International Baccalaureate Programme affects the school's entire population by building a positive academic focus, improving the general tone, and setting higher expectations among all students in the school. The popularity of the programme is certainly evident among the parents and teachers who took part in this study.

Figure 5.26. *The IB Programme is used to Attract New Students to the District*

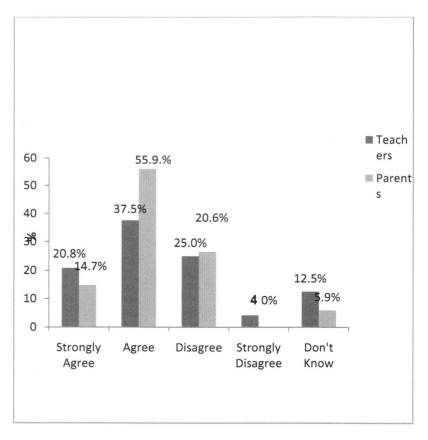

Summary of Political Implications and Effects

The findings of this study indicate that the political implications and effects addressed in the literature are, indeed, issues that frequently arise when discussing the International Baccalaureate Programme. The results of the surveys and interviews confirm that issues of opportunity, diversity, acceptance and sustainability are contentious issues which are woven into the fabric of the implementation and daily delivery of the International Baccalaureate Programme. It is important to be aware of these implications and effects and to develop creative and innovative ways to respond to and address these issues.

International Baccalaureate Demands on Human and
Physical Resources

This section summarizes the results of the findings related to the human and physical needs in a school with an International Baccalaureate Programme. It will look at some of the difficulties surrounding professional development and staffing. It will also look at the needs of the staff and the perspectives of the parents in regards to the physical resources already present in the school. The recommendations of the survey respondents on school resources will be reported as well.

Human Challenges
(Professional Development and Staffing)

The literature indicated the need for teachers to undertake specific professional development in order to teach International Baccalaureate courses (http://www.ibo.org). Results from the teacher survey indicated that most teachers felt that support was provided for International Baccalaureate Organization required activities in the form of financial assistance for course fees, travel and accommodation costs, and time off. Table 5.10 shows the results from the teacher surveys concerning the support provided for the required professional development.

Table 5.10

The school provides adequate support for required IBO professional development. Support is provided in the form of:

Category	Frequency	Percentage
Financial Assistance (course fees)	18	75.0
Financial Assistance (travel)	19	79.1
Time off	13	56.5

While teachers were generally of the opinion that the school district provided adequate financial support for the required International Baccalaureate Organization course fees, travel and accommodation costs, the findings indicate that teachers did not feel as strongly about receiving adequate amounts of time off. When looking at the data from this question, 56.5% of teachers agreed or strongly agreed that they received an adequate amount of time off, 26.1% disagreed or strongly disagreed with this statement, and 17.4% were unsure or did not know whether they received an adequate amount of time off.

There are challenges that arise concerning staffing of an International Baccalaureate school. More specifically, it can be difficult to find teachers and staff members who are willing to take the required International Baccalaureate professional development; finding those who are ready to think and teach "outside the box" and who are willing to take the extra responsibility and preparation that goes along with teaching International Baccalaureate courses. Many of the teachers interviewed expressed that "there are just not enough teachers interested in teaching in the IB programme" and "that many teachers experience burnout as a result of the incredible marking load and challenging curriculum that they must deliver." The majority of teachers surveyed indicated that if they had access to more money for IB programmes, they would put it into added staffing and professional development (95.2%). This is illustrated in Figure 5.27.

Figure 5.27. *Additional Money for IB Programmes Should Be Spent On X?*

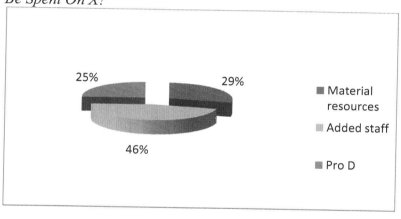

Resource Needs of the International Baccalaureate Programme

This section outlines the results of the findings related to the resources needed in an International Baccalaureate Programme. It reviews staff and parent perspectives on the adequacy of school equipment and resources. Since there was a lack of information in the literature on this topic, the study considered seven main resource areas identified as important through the personal experience of educators. The survey responses regarding recourses are reported in Table 5.11.

Table 5.11 *Mean Scores for Responses to Resources*

Resource Areas	Mean*	N	Mean*	n
Computers	2.77	22	3.00	25
Laptops	1.71	21	1.77	22
Library resources Periodicals/books	2.85	20	2.86	28
Internet media	3.10	20	3.00	26
Qualified Staff	3.38	24	3.38	29
Fine Arts Resources	2.89	9	2.75	20
Science Lab Resources	2.57	14	3.03	29

* Based on a scale where 1 = strongly disagree, 2 = disagree, 3 = agree and 4 = strongly agree. "Don't know" responses excluded from calculation of mean. The higher the mean, the greater is the level of agreement.

The Needs of Computers in International Baccalaureate Programmes

The survey focused on three main aspects for computer technology: computers, laptops, and internet media. When asked if there were sufficient school resources in the area of technology, there was not a consensus with the parents, as shown in Figure 5.28. While 50% stated there were sufficient resources, 21% disagreed and 24% did not know. With laptops there was a limited consensus as 62% either disagreed or strongly disagreed. The mean scores were 2.71 for computers, and the mean was only 1.77 for laptops. Teachers had mixed views, as 57% agreed they had sufficient computer resources while 33% disagreed or strongly disagreed (Figure 5.28). There was a consensus among teachers (75% disagree and strongly disagree) that there was insufficient access to laptops.

Figure 5.28. *Do IB Students Have Increased Access to Technology?*

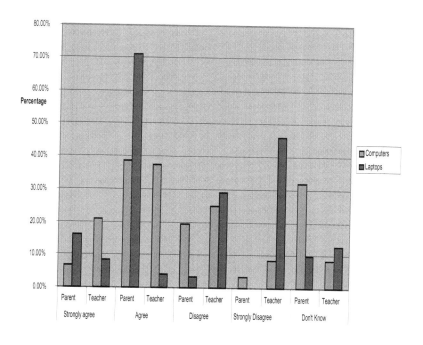

Other School Resources Required by International Baccalaureate Programmes

Parents and teachers were asked if they had sufficient resources in areas that included: libraries, qualified staff, fine arts, and science labs. Of notable significance was the Fine Arts category. A large number of people (62.3% of teachers, 45% of parents) did not know the status of this area. Parents' mean score was 2.75 and teacher's mean score was 2.89 (Table 5.12).

The resources provided by the library had a similar mean score for the parents and teachers with 2.85 and 2.86. There was a general consensus among teachers that the resources were sufficient but parents did not reach a consensus due to the lack of people who responded to the question (Table 5.12). When evaluating science lab resources, the parents had a general consensus, with 70% agreeing or strongly agreeing that the school had sufficient resources. On the other hand, teachers could not answer this question effectively as 62% did not know if there were sufficient resources in the sciences (Table 5.12).

Both teachers and parents responded with strong consensus that the schools had sufficient resources when it came to the school's teaching staff (Table 5.12). While many of the open-ended responses commented on the need for smaller class sizes, the survey instrument showed that the respective groups were satisfied with the current staffing situation.

Table 5.12
My School Has Sufficient Resources in the Following Areas

	Parents			Teachers		
Area	Mean Score	Consensus	Nf	Mean Score	Consensus	Nf
Library	2.86	46% No Consensus	28	2.85	67%- General Consensus	20
Science /lab	3.03	70%- general consensus	29	2.57	62% DK - No Consensus	14
Fine Arts	2.75	45% No Consensus	20	2.89	62.5% - DK No Consensus	9
Staff	3.38	85% Strong Consensus	29	3.38	95% - Strong Consensus	24

Based on a scale where 1=strongly disagree, 2=disagree, 3=agree, and 4=strongly agree. "Don't know" responses were excluded from the calculation of mean. The higher the mean, the greater is the level of agreement. Strong consensus is based on a score of 80% of respondents provided answers in adjacent categories (i.e. agree and strongly agree), lower or general consensus is 60% - 80% in adjacent categories, and no consensus is considered if less than 60%.

Parent and Teacher Recommendations for Resources

Survey respondents were asked to identify what programme areas they would invest additional money in if they could (Figure 5.29).

- Materials/resources
- Added staff
- Programs/development

For parents there was a consensus (88%) to invest in resources. For teachers, 61% wanted staff, and 38% wanted resources (Figure 5.29). Parents provided multiple suggestions for resource improvement: computer resources/media, better trained staff, library materials (periodicals, books), fine art resources. The teachers overwhelmingly identified "smaller class sizes" as a key resource item. This study clearly identifies the importance of diverse resources and appropriate staffing to accommodate the International Baccalaureate Programme's needs.

Figure 4.30. *Where Would You Put More Money?*

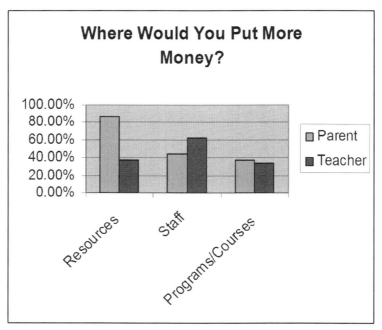

Multiple Responses, so percentages may exceed 100%

Final Thoughts about Findings

The International Baccalaureate Programme opens new academic avenues for students. The findings of this study show that the International Baccalaureate Program meets the needs of those exceptional students who require a more challenging curriculum and are self-motivated to succeed. The programme definitely meets the academic needs of students. It meets and or exceeds local requirements for promotion and provides a more than adequate preparation for entrance into leading universities. The programme offers equal opportunity to all self-motivated and academically capable students.

Despite the emerging evidence that the International Baccalaureate Programme is a positive element for a host school, this study demonstrates that there remains a significant lack of understanding about the impact, potential benefits, and potential pitfalls of the programme among key stakeholders. Many respondents were unclear of the academic requirements for International Baccalaureate students. There was considerable discrepancy between answers to similar questions. Participants were uncertain if the programme better met the needs of students than other programs and while all participants were very positive and confident that the programme was a good one, they often had a difficult time articulating why.

The impact of the International Baccalaureate programme on the students, staff, and school is multifaceted. The findings of this research indicate that:

- There is evidence of strong leadership, motivation, competitiveness, and cliques among students in the International Baccalaureate Programme.
- Students who are currently involved in the program express evidence of strong interest in it.
- There is strong interest from other students in the school about the International Baccalaureate Programme. Pre-IB programmes for grade 10 students offer courses for students wishing to be accepted into the programme.
- The IB programme is used to attract new students to the school.

- The atmosphere in schools with IB programmes tends to be positive and learning based.
- Teachers believe that the programme addresses the needs of students who desire an academic challenge.
- Teachers feel that the programme is of benefit to the general population in terms of setting high expectations and standards, as well as instilling an academic based focus in the school.
- Parents perceive that the International Baccalaureate Programme has a positive effect on the school, yet are often unclear as to the reasons why they feel this way.

Chapter 6
So, what does this all mean?

This chapter outlines the resulting conclusions and recommendations that emerged from my evaluation of the IB programme. The first section presents the conclusions that emerged from this study. The second offers recommendations for general policy and practice. The third section offers recommendations for the North Vancouver School District. The fourth section offers ideas for further research.

Conclusions

The major conclusions that emerged from the study are presented in this section by addressing the specific research questions. The themes of academics, economics, politics, and culture are addressed through these questions.

Do International Baccalaureate Programmes meet the academic needs of students?

This research study agrees with current literature and suggests that International Baccalaureate Programmes at the high school level do indeed meet the academic requirements of students. Both teachers and parents involved with the programmes at Sir Winston Churchill and Britannia Community Secondary School concur when considering the academic requirements and needs of students and schools. The high school level programme meets the academic needs of students.

Does the International Baccalaureate Programme fit into the local aim or goal of education?

The Canadian Ministry of Education states that the purpose of the British Columbia school system is to enable learners to develop their individual potential and to acquire the knowledge, skills and attitudes needed to contribute to a healthy society and a prosperous and sustainable economy. The International Baccalaureate Programme fits within this provincial goal. It is a complete and rigorous curriculum designed to prepare students for entrance into the world's leading universities. The research undertaken at Britannia and Churchill has shown that parents and teachers certainly agree that the International Baccalaureate meets the local aims of education. International Baccalaureate students are getting into post-secondary institutions at a much higher rate than non-IB students. The principal purpose of the programme is to provide students with a balanced, integrated curriculum that focuses on all academic areas. This study has shown that parents and teachers agree that the programme provides a challenging curriculum. International Baccalaureate students are provided opportunities to demonstrate their commitment to learning while developing the discipline necessary for university and life success. Students are responsible for committing to the programme, developing international understanding, and demonstrating responsible citizenship. Parents and teachers enthusiastically agree that all courses in the programme require university level work that meets and surpasses the requirements of their local school boards of education. In fact, my research showed that parents and teachers agreed that the International Baccalaureate Programme better meets the academic need of students than does the provincial curriculum. In order to receive an International Baccalaureate Diploma, students must take and pass world standard exams in six subject areas, fulfill a community service requirement, submit an extended essay, and follow an interdisciplinary course in Theory of Knowledge. These requirements generally meet and or exceed the requirements of the schools studied.

The Primary Years Program and the Middle Years Programme are early in their development and, as a result, have few definitive studies of evaluation to support them. While the limited literature suggests that both programmes adequately meet the academic needs of students, this study cannot offer additional data in support of these claims. My original research plan included an examination of the Primary Years Programme and Middle Years Programme at Stratford Hall, the only school in British Columbia offering the programmes. Unfortunately, my request to interview and survey teachers and parents at Stratford Hall was denied. Due to the unfortunate limitations of this particular study, I am unable to adequately comment on the academic merits of the Primary Years Programme and the Middle Years Programme offered by the International Baccalaureate Organization.

Is the notion of 'best practice' the driving philosophy behind the initiative?

This study revealed a consensus among the teacher participants on the ability of the International Baccalaureate to offer challenging coursework, specialized courses, a focus on skill development, and an opportunity for university credit. All of these areas can be characterized as 'good educational practice.' Furthermore, the interview respondents from both Britannia and Churchill Secondary responded favourably when describing the International Baccalaureate programme. The programme offers an additional choice for students looking to pursue a more rigorous academic curriculum that would better prepare them for post secondary education.

Is the driving force behind the implementation of an International Baccalaureate Programme solely that of attracting students (money) to the school district?

The evidence provided by this study demonstrates that the emphasis and focus of the International Baccalaureate Programmes of Britannia and Churchill is the curriculum itself and not on attracting students to the school district. In fact, the extra costs attached to both International Baccalaureate Programmes were incurred by the school and school district and not the student, thereby excluding the financial incentive as a legitimate driving force behind the implementation of the International Baccalaureate Programmes at Churchill and Britannia.

What measures of accountability are enforced in an International Baccalaureate school?

The research undertaken in this project suggests that there are many levels of accountability in an International Baccalaureate school, ranging from individual student accountability to accountability by the worldwide International Baccalaureate Organization. The following conclusions summarize the levels of accountability evident at both Churchill and Britannia Secondary Schools in Vancouver, British Columbia.

The International Baccalaureate Programme is a comprehensive and rigorous curriculum designed to prepare students for a quality university education. The primary objective of the International Baccalaureate Programme is to provide students with a balanced, integrated curriculum in all academic areas. Students who excel in the International Baccalaureate Programme demonstrate a strong commitment to learning and develop the discipline necessary to succeed later in life. Students in the International Baccalaureate Programme are responsible for making a commitment to the programme, developing international understanding and demonstrating responsible citizenship. Students in the programme are personally accountable for their studies and success in the programme. To receive an International Baccalaureate Diploma, students must take and pass world standard exams in six subject areas, fulfill a community service requirement, submit an extended essay, and follow an interdisciplinary course in Theory of Knowledge.

Teachers working in the International Baccalaureate Programme are accountable on two different levels. First, they are responsible for taking additional courses, workshops and professional development provided by the International Baccalaureate Organization. This training allows the teachers to become knowledgeable about the expectations, curriculum, and methodology prescribed by the International Baccalaureate Organization. Second, teachers are accountable for teaching the curriculum laid out by the IBO, and adequately preparing their students for the International Baccalaureate exams in each of the six subject areas.

At the school level, a team of individuals (including the IB coordinator and the administrative staff) are accountable on many different levels. They are accountable for student admissions, scheduling of courses, hiring staff, teacher training, and the daily running of the programme. In addition they are responsible for ensuring the internal assessment of student work, liaising with parent and community, and the proper preparation of students for exams.

The International Baccalaureate Organization (IBO) is also accountable for the International Baccalaureate Programme. The IBO provides International Baccalaureate schools with detailed curriculum guidelines for each programme and subject area. They also provide teacher training workshops. In addition, the IBO completes external assessment of diploma students' work, and procedures for school-based (internal) assessment of student work. The IBO is also responsible for the administration and grading of IBO examinations. The grading system for the exams is criterion-referenced. This means that each student's performance is measured against well-defined levels of achievement. Top grades reflect knowledge and skills relative to set standards applied equally to all schools. Responsibility for all academic judgments about the quality of students' work rests with over 5,000 examiners worldwide, led by chief examiners with international authority in their fields. At another level the IBO works closely with schools throughout the initial authorization process by offering introductory workshops and supplying schools with application forms. During the process of implementing an International Baccalaureate Programme, which is required for authorization, the IBO advises schools on the materials that they will need and offer teacher training workshops and conferences (IBO, 2004).

As it can be evidenced from the levels of accountability discussed above, there are many measures in place that ensure that the International Baccalaureate Programme is implemented, delivered, and assessed fairly and equitably.

What are the effects of an International Baccalaureate Programme on student populations?

This research project confirms current research literature and agrees that there is a definite impact upon the students and the school by the International Baccalaureate Programme. The host school is affected through daily culture but not through the physical infrastructure.

A major concern at the beginning this research was to determine if International Baccalaureate students are segregated from the rest of the school population. While the notion of a school within a school exists, it does not have to become the case in all scenarios. There are numerous opportunities for International Baccalaureate students to participate in school wide leadership opportunities and to be involved with the daily activities of the general student population. The curriculum provides avenues for students to become involved and play major roles in areas like student council. Overall students involved in the programme appear to be aware and driven individuals who have opportunities to become part of an integrated school community.

Physically, International Baccalaureate host schools remain very similar to non-International Baccalaureate schools. The research suggests that little or no change in physical resources is detectable with the exception of added computer usage for the programme. The International Baccalaureate Programme enhances the academic focus of a school and provides additional opportunities for a unique segment of the school population.

Recommendations for Policy and Practice

The vast majority of those individuals involved in International Baccalaureate Programmes are strong supporters of the programme. The International

Baccalaureate is a good option for the gifted population. It meets the academic needs of an underserved segment of the student population, but it is not a program for all students or teachers. Interested districts should conduct further research in the Primary and Middle Years Programmes, International Baccalaureate Programmes in other districts, and other academic programmes like Advanced Placement before making a final decision.

With particular consideration to North Vancouver, the district should reflect upon its goals and reasons for implementing an International Baccalaureate Programme. Specifically, it is important to establish good lines of communication with teachers, staff, students, and community members prior to implementation of this type of programme. In order to avoid isolation, student leadership opportunities that combine International Baccalaureate and mainstream students must be developed in advance.

Site specifically, it is necessary to hire a full time International Baccalaureate coordinator for the school in order to promote the programme to the community either through direct means (newspaper ads) or indirectly. Additionally, there ought to be a common area where International Baccalaureate students can work together and have sufficient technology to ensure access to resources.

Recommendations for Further Research

The following are suggestions identified as areas in need of further research:

Districts considering an International Baccalaureate Programme should conduct an in depth study on the actual classroom needs of an International Baccalaureate class. It would be valuable to schools to have access to a specific list of teacher, student, and building requirements prior to beginning the process of becoming an International

Baccalaureate school. Additionally, a comparison of an International Baccalaureate classroom and a provincially examinable classroom should be conducted. Through this comparison, schools can look at whether the teaching styles differ greatly from one classroom to the next. This examination would allow schools and districts to come to a conclusion about whether or not the training for International Baccalaureate teachers is helpful and a worthwhile expenditure.

Advanced Placement and International Baccalaureate Programmes ought to be compared. This additional study would determine if one program is better to local implementation and marketing than the other. A combined study of International Baccalaureate graduates and individuals who have dropped out or withdrawn from the programme ought to be performed. As a result, the effect of stress and burnout on International Baccalaureate participants could possibly be determined.

References

Ball, S.J., Vincent, C. & Radnor, H. (1997). Into confusion: LEAs, accountability and Democracy. *Journal of Education Policy, 12*(3), pp.147-63.

Bangall, N. (1997) Un Mariage de convenance! The International Baccalaureate and the French Baccalaureat Professionel. What Chance of a Union. *International Education-e*. 3, 17-21. Retrieved November 4, 2004 from http://www.services.canberra.edu

Brayne, R. (2004). *Choice in the North Vancouver School District.*

Brown, D.J., (2004). School choice under open enrollment. Grant awarded by the Society for the Advancement of Excellence in Education, Kelowna, B.C.Retrieved October 1, 2004 from www.saee.ca

Codrington, S. (2004). Applying the concept of best practice to international schools. *Journal of Research in International Education,* Vol. 3(2), p.173-188.

College Board. (2004). The Advanced Placement Programme. Retrieved October 31, 2004 from http://apcentral.collegeboard.com/

Criticisms of the AP and IB programmes-advanced placement, international baccalaureate-brief article. (2002). *Gifted Child Today Magazine, Summer 2002* Retrieved October 27, 2004, from http://www.findarticles.com/p/articles/mi_m0HRV/is_3_25/ai_90162359

Daniel, N. & Cox, J. (1985). Providing options for superior students in secondary schools. *NASSP Bulletin, 69,* 25-30.

Daniel, N. & Cox, J. (1992). International education for high-ability students: an avenue to excellence. *NASSP Bulletin, April.*

Eilber, C.R. & Warshaw, S.J. (1988). North Carolina school of science and mathematics: The special environment within a statewide science high school. In P.E. Brandwein & A.H. Passos (Eds.), *Gifted young in science: Potential through performance* (pp. 201-207). Washington DC: National Science Teachers Association.

Freeman, I. (1987). The international baccalaureate. *The College Board Review, 5-6,* 40.

Gehring, J. (2001). The international baccalaureate: "Cadillac" of college-prep programmes. *Education Week, 32,* 19.

Glanz, J. (1998). *Action Research: An Educational Guide to School Improvement.* Norwoods, MA: Christopher Gordon.

Gollub, J.P., Bertenthal, M.W., Labov, J.B. Curtis, & P.C. (Eds). (2002). *Learning and understanding: improving advanced study of mathematics and science in us high schools, committee on programmes for advanced study of mathematics and science in American high schools.* Washington DC: National Academy of Sciences.

Hargrove, K. (2003). If you build it, they will come. *Gifted Child Today,* Vol 26(1), p.30.

Hayden, Mary C. & Wong, Cynthia S.D. (1997). *International Education and Cultural Preservation.* Bath, U.K: Carfax Publishing Ltd.

Hill, P. (1996). The educational consequences of choice. *Phi Delta Kappan, 77(10),* 671-680.

Hinrichs, J. (2003). A comparison of levels of international understanding among students of the International Baccalaureate diploma and Advanced Placement programmes in the USA. *Journal of Research in International Education,* Vol. 2(3), p.331-348.

Hittleman, D.R., & Simon, A.J. (2002). *Interpreting Educational Research: An Introduction for Consumers of Research 3rd ed.* Upper Saddle River, New Jersey: Merrill Prentice Hall.

Hoy, W., & Tarter, C. (2004). *Administrators Solving the Problems of Practice.* Boston, MA: Pearson.

International Baccalaureate and the University of Alberta. (2004). University of Alberta. Retrieved November 10, 2004 from http://www.registrar.ualberta.ca/ro.cfm?id=261

International Baccalaureate Organization (2004). *Workshops Schedule and Registration Materials.*

International Baccalaureate Organization (2004). *A basis for Practice: the Primary Years Programme.* Retrieved October 31, 2004 from

http://www.ibo.org/ibo/index.cfm?contentid=7EB3
9840-C56F-98A0-
67A9C7127EAD217D&method=display&language
=EN

International Baccalaureate Organization (2004). *IBNA
Student Survey 2003 Presentation.* Retrieved
October 31, 2004 from
http://www.ibnasubregional.org/Initiatives.html

International Baccalaureate Organization and the College
Board. (2002). *Informational Brochure on IB and
AP.* Retrieved October 31, 2004 from
http://www.ibo.org/ibo/index.cfm?contentid=0000E
614-48A3-1DD5-
8E1280C12645FD37&method=display&language=
EN

International Baccalaureate Organization. (2003). *IB North
America University Guide to the IB Diploma
Programme.* Retrieved October 31, 2004 from
http://www.ibo.org/ibo/index.cfm?contentid=00037
59F-B616-1DCF-
BF7080C12645FC87&method=display&language=
EN

Leithwood, K., Edge, K. & Jantzi, D. (1999). *Educational
Accountability: The state of the art.* Gutersloh:
Bertelsmann Foundation.

Lichten, William. (2000). Whither Advanced Placement?
Education Policy Analysis Archives, 8, 29.
Retrieved October 10, 2004 from
http://epaa.asu.edu/epaa/v8n29.html

Macpherson, R.J.S., Cibulka, J.G., Monk, D.H., & Wong, K.K. (1997). Introduction to the politics of accountability: Challenges in retrospect. In R.J.S. Macpherson (ed.) *The politics of accountability: educative and international perspectives,* pp. 1-12. Thousand Oaks, California: Corwin Press.

Mathison, S. & Ross, W.E. (2004). *The hegemony of accountability in schools and universities. Workplace Features.*

Matthews, Jay. (2003, June 2). 100 Best high schools in America. *Newsweek, 141*, 48-54.

Miles, M.B, and Huberman, A.M. (1994). *Qualitative Data Analysis,* 2nd Ed., p. 10-12. Newbury Park, CA: Sage.

National Research Council. (2002). *Learning and understanding: improving advanced study of mathematics and science in u.s. high schools: report of the content panel for chemistry*. National Research Council. Retrieved October 15, 2004 from http://books.nap.edu/books/NI000403/html/

National Science Foundation (1997). *User-friendly handbook for mixed method evaluations*. Retrieved December 7, 2004 from http://www.ehr.nsf.gov/EHR/REC/pubs/NSF97-153/start.htm

North Vancouver School District (1993). *Proposal to establish a district international baccalaureate programme.*

North Vancouver School District (2003). *Report of November 8ᵗʰ community forum.*

North Vancouver School District (2004). *Policies and regulations.*

Osborne, K. (1999). *Education: A guide to the Canadian school debate- or, who wants what and why?* Toronto: Penguin Books.

Pajak, E. (2000). *Approaches to clinical supervision: alternatives for improving instruction.* Norwood, MA: Christopher-Gordon Publishers, Inc.

Paris, P. (2003). The International Baccalaureate: A case study on why students choose to do the IB. *International Education* Journal, 4, 232-243. Retrieved October, 2004, from http://iej.cjb.net

Peterson, A.D.C. (1987). *Schools Across Frontiers.* La Salle, IL: Open Court.

Poelzer, G. (1997). An Empirical Study of the Achievement of International Baccalaureate Students in Biology, Chemistry, and Physics- in Alberta. *Journal of Secondary Gifted Education.* 8, 28p. Retrieved October 5, 2004 from Academic Search Primer Database http://clearx.library.ubc.ca

Poelzer, G. (1997). The International Baccalaureate: A programme for gifted and talented secondary students. *Roeper Review.* 19, 4p. Retrieved September 11, 2004, from Academic Search Primer Database http://Search.epnet.com

Poelzer, G.H. & Feldhusen, J.F. An empirical study of the achievement of international baccalaureate students in biology, chemistry, and physics- in Alberta. *Journal of Secondary Gifted Education, 8*, 28.

Poelzer, G.H. (1994). An empirical study of international baccalaureate students in the sciences. (Doctoral dissertation, Purdue University, 1994). *Dissertation Abstracts International, 55*, 2337.

Potter, D. & Hayden, M. (2004). Parental choice in the Buenos Aires bilingual school market. *Journal of Research in International Education,* Vol. 3(1), p. 87-111.

Poulson, L. (1998). Accountability, teacher professionalism and education reform in England. *Teacher Development,* 2(3), p.419-31.

Raptis, H. & Fleming, T. (2003). Effective instruction, part II: An analysis of general research findings and specific findings for diverse learners and subjects, p. 1-26.

Renaud, G. (1974). *Experimental period of the international baccalaureate: Objectives and results.* Paris: Unesco Press.

Richmond School District (2001). *School Choice: setting the stage for a productive discussion.*

Robertson, J.E. (2003). Teachers' perceptions of accountability at an international school. *Journal of Research in International Education,* Vol. 2(3), p. 277-300.

Ryan, J. and Heise, M. (2002). The political economy of school choice. *Yale Law Journal, 111, 1-95.*

Savage, David. (May 1982). "The International Baccalaureate Challenges High School Students." *Educational Leadership.*

Schofield, J. (1999). Reach for the top. *Maclean's.* Vol. 112 (50), p.90-3.

Sergiovanni, T., & Starratt, R. (2002). *Supervision: A Redefinition.* New York, NY: McGraw-Hill.

Singh, N. (2002). Becoming International. *Educational Leadership,* 60, 5p. Retrieved September 21, 2004, from EBSCO Research Database http://web14.epnet.com/citation.asp

Sjogren, C. & Campbell, P. (2003). The International Baccalaureate: A diploma of Quality, depth, and breadth. *College and University Journal, Fall 2003,* Vol. 79(2), p. 55-8.

Smedley, D. (1995). Marketing secondary schools to parents: Some lessons from the research on parental choice. *Educational Management and Administration,* 23(2),p.96-103

Stanley, J.C. & Benbow, C.P. (1982). Educating mathematically precious youths: Twelve policy recommendations. *Educational Researcher, 11,* 4-9.

Stratford Hall (2004). *Programme Student Profile.* Retrieved October 22, 2004 http://www.stratfordhall.bc.ca/Programme/StudentProfile.htm

Stratford Hall (2004). *Welcome To Stratford Hall.* Retrieved October 22, 2004 from http://www.stratfordhall.bc.ca/

Taylor, Lyn; Poegrebin, Mark; & Dodge, Mary. (Dec. 2002). Advanced Placement Advanced Pressures: Academic Dishonesty Among Elite High School Students. *Educational Studies 33*(4), pp. 403-419.

Thomas, P.B. (1998). Students across frontiers. *Journal of College Admissions, 121*, 7-14.

Tookey, M. (1999). The International Baccalaureate. *Journal of Secondary Gifted Education.* 11, 52. Retrieved September 11, 2004, from Academic Search Primer Database http://Search.epnet.com

Tookey, Mary Enda. (Winter 99/2000). "The International Baccalaureate." Journal of Secondary Gifted Education; 11(2), 52.

University of Alberta. (2004). *Early Admission and Transfer Credit for IB Students.* Retrieved November 10, 2004 from http://www.registrar.ualberta.ca/ro.cfm?id=966

University of British Columbia. (2004). *Welcome: Admissions Requirements: International Baccalaureate.* (2004).. Retrieved November 10, 2004 from http://students.ubc.ca/welcome/admission.cfm?page=ib

U.S. Department of Education. (1999). *Answers in the Toolbox: Academic Intensity, Attendance Patterns,* and *Bachelor's Degree Attainment*. Jessup, MD: Clifford Adelman.

Vancouver School Board. (2004). *Schools*. Retrieved November 22, 2004 from http://www.vsb.bc.ca/schools/default.htm

Viteritti, J. (1996). Stacking the deck for the poor: the new politics of school choice. *Brookings Review, 14(3), 10-17.*

Appendix A: About the Author

Edward L. Varner, AKA Spaghetti Eddie, has been an educator, a musician, a freelance percussionist, actor, and arts education specialist and advocate for more than 20 years. His collection of original and educational folk songs has inspired children and their parents for many years. He has taught award winning K-12 music programs in California, Nevada, and Washington, presented workshops for the International Reading Association, National Association for Elementary School Principals, Hawaii International Conference on Education, Washington State OSPI, and led many district in-services. He is currently the Supervisor of Music Education for the Great Falls Public Schools in Great Falls, Montana.

Ed completed the Master's Degree in Educational Administration in 2005 from the University of British Columbia and is currently working towards a Doctorate of Education in Educational Leadership and Administration at Concordia University, Chicago.

As an educator, I have always been a firm believer in the philosophies of integration, diversification, and differentiation of curriculum to better meet the needs of students. I must know my students in order to adequately and effectively meet them where they are and help them progress to the next level. This philosophy of knowing your students necessitates the added element of care. Educators must care for their students, themselves, and have the fortitude to continue caring when it appears that others have surrendered. - Edward Varner

Made in the USA
Lexington, KY
16 May 2013